FACTS & FABRICATIONS
Unraveling the History of
QUILTS & SLAVERY

■ **8 Projects** ■ **20 Blocks** ■ **First-Person Accounts**

BARBARA BRACKMAN

C&T PUBLISHING

Text and Artwork © 2006 by Barbara Brackman

Publisher: Amy Marson

Editorial Director: Gailen Runge

Acquisitions Editor: Jan Grigsby

Editor: Deb Rowden

Technical Editors: Robyn Gronning, Cynthia Keyes Hilton

Copyeditor/Proofreader: Wordfirm Inc.

Design Director/Cover & Book Designer: Christina D. Jarumay

Illustrator: Tim Manibusan

Production Assistant: Matt Allen

Photography: studio shots by Jon Blumb, landscape shots by Barbara Brackman

Published by C&T Publishing, Inc., P.O. Box 1456, Lafayette, CA 94549

Front cover: *Checkedy Cloth Sampler* designed by Barbara Brackman, pieced by Pamela Mayfield, machine quilted by Rosie Mayhew

Back cover: *Sweet Chariot* by Jean A. Wells

Library of Congress Cataloging-in-Publication Data

Brackman, Barbara.
 Barbara Brackman's facts & fabrications: unraveling the history of quilts and slavery : 8 projects - 20 blocks - first-person accounts / Barbara Brackman.
  p. cm.
 Includes bibliographical references and index.
 ISBN-13: 978-1-57120-364-9 (paper trade : alk. paper)
 ISBN-10: 1-57120-364-8 (paper trade : alk. paper)
 1. Quilting--Patterns. 2. Patchwork--Patterns. 3. Slavery–Southern States–History. I. Title. II. Title: Barbara Brackman's facts and fabrications. III. Title: Facts & fabrications.
 TT835.B638 2006
 746.46'041--dc22
                    2006013689

Printed in China

10 9 8 7 6 5 4 3 2 1

Acknowledgments

Thanks, as always, to photographer Jon Blumb, who took the studio photographs, and to editor Deb Rowden, who shaped the book into final form.

I am always indebted to the women who sew the quilts, especially Jean Stanclift and Pam Mayfield, who take my designs and add their own sense of order and taste to some rather sketchy ideas.

I taught this book as a class at Prairie Point Quilts in Shawnee, Kansas, and I am grateful to the students who finished projects in time for photography. Without them, there would be no book. Thanks to Gloria Clark, Barbara Fife, Carol Kirchhoff, Dorothy LeBoeuf, Paula Mariedaughter, Linda Birch Mooney, Ilyse Moore, Mary Louise Pick, Jeanne Poore, Diane Weber, Jean Wells, and Lavon Wynn and to other friends who loaned quilts to be included.

I spent two years reading first-person accounts and looking at photographs to educate myself about slavery and African-American history. I am grateful to the many librarians, archivists, and museum personnel who have collected the material and made it available. The book wouldn't have been possible without the Library of Congress online archive. It is indeed a national treasure.

And thanks to my friend Cuesta Benberry, who got me interested in the topic. When I write, she is always the reader I have in mind.

table

Like other myths, however, these stories will survive because they help define our culture. At the turn of the twenty-first century, Americans are eager to discuss Black History. Quilts and the Underground Railroad are the perfect pair of bookends for chronicles of slavery. The story of black heroes risking their lives for freedom and white heroes risking their liberty to shelter escaping slaves has resounding appeal. American studies professor James Horton noted, "With the Underground Railroad, you have a real Hollywood story. Everyone gets to be a hero."[4]

Harriet Tubman Leading a Family to Freedom by Michael Cummings, New York City, 2004. Photograph by Karen Bell.

Michael Cummings was commissioned by the National Underground Railroad Freedom Center to create a quilt. His quilt has layers of meaning, much of which the viewer can easily interpret. The imagery is a literal telling of Harriet Tubman's story. In an interview, Cummings said he "wanted to create figures that would engage viewers of all ages, images that viewers could identify with."[5]

Symbolism works most effectively when both the artist and the audience are familiar with the meaning of the image. Many Americans know that escaping slaves navigated by the North Star. However, some imagery is more difficult to interpret. Without Cummings' words to guide us, we don't know why he chose the pieced border pattern. There may be no underlying message; however, part of the enjoyment of looking at the piece is speculating as to its meaning. Art is often a silent dialogue between artist and audience.

Harriet Tubman and the Underground Railroad by Terry Clothier Thompson, Lawrence, Kansas, 1999. 78″ × 90″.

Terry Thompson loves using quilt pattern names to construct a metaphorical story. In this quilt honoring Harriet Tubman, she chose Union Star, Slave Chain, and Underground Railroad blocks to create a narrative easily read by quiltmakers who are also familiar with the blocks. Other symbolism is so personal that we can only understand it by reading the words in her published pattern. The Dogtooth strip in the upper left, for example, recalls how slave owners used dogs to track escapees. The Snail's Trail design below the Nine-Patch blocks refers to slave-tilled gardens.

Because we know today's quilt artists express ideas through symbolism, we tend to look at nineteenth-century quilts with the same eye. There is very little evidence of nineteenth-century quiltmakers using pattern names symbolically. In fact, only a few of the names that we take for granted today were used in the nineteenth century.

This book, then, offers today's quiltmakers an alternative framework to weave an accurate history of slavery into their quilts. From my _Encyclopedia of Pieced Quilt Patterns,_ an index to 4,000 blocks, I chose twenty poetic names to represent twenty chapters in the story from Africa to Reconstruction. Names like Catch Me If You Can, Lincoln's Platform, and Lost Ship are perfect for symbolizing various events, but it is important to emphasize that these patterns have _no_ historical connection to slave-made quilts. In many cases, quilts in these designs did not appear until the 1930s, when quiltmaking was a popular feature in newspapers around the country.[6]

We can look at my pattern choices as an exercise in poetic license. Every artist knows the importance of symbolism in personal expression. Quilt pattern names are a form of poetry—imagery that can evoke the past and words that can add layers of symbolic meaning to a quilt's visual beauty. In this book, I present ideas for using pattern names, as well as color and fabric style, to create quilts that symbolize the story of slavery and freedom.

I am also giving you a poetic license (suitable for photo-copying and framing to hang over your sewing machine). It's something you really don't need. Everyone is born with one, but having a paper certificate may encourage you to exercise your creativity more freely. Do read the fine print, however, which notes that your own poetic license doesn't give you rights to interpret another quilter's symbolism as history. You cannot use it to read a "map" into a nineteenth-century Nine-Patch or interpret a Log Cabin design as a code. Poetry is poetry; history is history. Mix the facts and fabrications in your own quilts if you like, but don't make the mistake of confusing fiction or myth for American history.

Slavery and Freedom: 1619–1964

A Time Line of

1619 Africans first brought to American colonies.

1641 Massachusetts legalizes slavery. Other colonies follow.

1776 The Society of Friends (Quakers) in Pennsylvania orders members to free their slaves.

1777 Vermont outlaws slavery.

1780 Judges in Massachusetts determine that the state constitution, which declares all men as free and equal, outlaws slavery. A Pennsylvania law passes that says all slaves born after a set date will be freed on their 28th birthday. Other Northern states follow with "gradual emancipation" laws over the next 25 years.

1807 The United States abolishes the slave trade, meaning no new captives may be brought to America. This law takes effect in 1808. During the previous decade, 200,000 Africans had been imported.

1817 The American Colonization Society is founded, with the goal of returning freed slaves to Africa.

1820 Congress agrees to bar slavery from new territories and states north of the Mason-Dixon Line.

1822 Liberia is founded as a colony in Africa for former slaves.

1831 The radical abolitionist newspaper, *The Liberator*, begins publication in Boston and demands an immediate end to slavery.

1833 The American Anti-Slavery Society is founded, with the goal of immediately freeing all U.S. slaves.

1838 Great Britain abolishes slavery in all British colonies.

1839 The *Amistad,* an illegal slave ship taken over by its captives, is detained outside New York City.

1850 Congress passes the Fugitive Slave Law, requiring free states to hand over escaped slaves to former owners.

1852 Harriet Beecher Stowe publishes *Uncle Tom's Cabin* as a magazine serial, awakening many Americans to slavery's injustices.

1854 Congress decides residents of Kansas Territory can vote on whether this Northern state will be free or slave, prompting immigration by abolitionists and pro-slavery activists. Events in "Bleeding Kansas" affect the political party system, resulting in the birth of the Republican Party and uniting advocates of free territories.

1857 In the *Dred Scott* decision, the U.S. Supreme Court declares that African-Americans have no legal rights.

1859 In an effort to begin a slave revolt, antislavery activist John Brown and followers attack a federal arsenal in Harper's Ferry, Virginia, increasing tensions between North and South.

1860 In response to Republican Abraham Lincoln's election as president, South Carolina secedes from the United States.

1861 Eleven Southern states form the Confederacy. Civil War begins in April.

1862 Congress abolishes slavery in the District of Columbia.

1863 The Emancipation Proclamation frees slaves in seceded Confederate states.

1865 After the four-year Civil War ends with a treaty at Appomattox in April, the Thirteenth Amendment to the Constitution abolishes slavery in the United States.

1866 The Fourteenth Amendment extends citizenship rights to African-Americans.

1870 The Fifteenth Amendment, guaranteeing black Americans the right to vote, is ratified.

1875 Congress passes Civil Rights Acts, prohibiting some discrimination, laws with no effects in schools.

1877 Reconstruction ends as the federal government withdraws troops protecting African-Americans in the South.

1879 Exodusters begin migration from the South to the western states.

1881 Jim Crow laws (legal segregation) begin with Tennessee authorizing segregated railroad cars. Many other states follow by segregating all types of services.

1883 The U.S. Supreme Court overturns the Civil Rights Act, thus sanctioning segregation.

1896 In *Plessy v. Ferguson,* the U.S. Supreme Court sanctions the concept of "separate but equal" facilities.

1936–1940 Interviews of slaves and descendants are conducted by the Works Project Administration (WPA) Folklore Project.

1954 In *Brown v. Board of Education,* the U.S. Supreme Court overturns the idea of segregated schools.

1964 Congress passes the Civil Rights Act, outlawing discrimination. As Congresswoman Barbara Jordan said in 1974, "Through the process of amendment, interpretation, and court decision, I have finally been included in 'We, the people.' "

CHAPTER 2

Quilts and Slavery: A Historical Search

Women living in slavery made quilts. The statement seems obvious—quiltmaking was a common pastime of women throughout the country after 1800, but have we historical evidence?

The question is easy to answer because a surprisingly large body of supporting evidence survives. We can examine first-hand accounts, public records, and the actual objects. Many quilts in museums and private collections have been passed down with family stories that they were made by slaves. To use these quilts as evidence that enslaved people stitched quilts, we must first eliminate quilts made after 1865. A quilt made by a woman who was once in slavery is no evidence that slaves made quilts. Because the end of the Civil War marked the beginning of new design ideas as well as new technology, categorizing antique quilts as pre-war and postwar is relatively easy. Yet too many examples of so-called slave-made quilts are misdated—pieced from later fabrics and made in styles such as crazy quilts, usually attributed to the years after emancipation.

Once we've eliminated quilts made after 1865, we still have many quilts with credible family stories that they were made by enslaved women and passed on in families—either the makers' or the slave owners'. In 2000, Sotheby's auctions offered an appliquéd quilt made by a man nick-named "Yellow Bill" as a gift for the plantation family's 1852 wedding. The Maryland Historical Society owns a quilt donated in 1945 that was made a century earlier by a "midwife, possibly a slave," for the Calvert family.[7]

Unknown family, possibly in Texas, about 1910. We can date the photograph by the clothing the family wears, which shows styles fashionable in the early twentieth century. The strip quilt that hangs behind them, although a utility bedcover, also follows fashion. Among the clues to the date is the quilting style (usually called fans today), which was quite popular all over the South between 1880 and 1950.

Two-sided Log Cabin quilt, maker unknown, possibly from Oklahoma, 1925–1950, collection of Bob and Jan Nitcher. This quilt was purchased from an African-American woman in Tulsa. We assume she or a member of her family made it. Quilts made by African-Americans after slavery are rather common in terms of numbers, although this two-sided piece is uncommonly graphic.

Diaries and letters written by plantation-owning families support the evidence in surviving quilts. Right before the Civil War, Keziah Brevard often noted the activities of her personal servant in her diary: "Dorcas has commenced a quilt. I've gave her the scraps." That same month, Martha Watkins, living in slavery in Mississippi, asked her mistress to forward a dictated note describing recent social events: "We had a fine time last night with just our own people and Payton to play the violin and banjo, and Simon played on the tambourine. Susan had a quilting and after we got the quilt out they had to dance instead of a supper … I will have my quilting next Saturday night."[8]

Such contemporary references to quilts pieced and quilted for the slaves' own use are rare, but they are supported by memories collected during the Great Depression. The Works Progress Administration (WPA), a federal program, sponsored a Federal Writer's Project to give work to unemployed writers. Within that program was a Folklore Project, which hired writers to gather stories of Americans who had lived through remarkable times. Interviewers talked to old cowboys, former factory workers, and people raised in Indian Territory. The largest group interviewed was made up of former slaves, who were asked a set of questions that occasionally led to talk of quilt memories.[9]

Georgia Flournoy of Eufaula, Alabama was interviewed about 1938 by the Works Progress Administration (WPA). A good deal of the information collected in the federal documentation projects is available at the Library of Congress' website, giving us much information about African American history. Photo courtesy of the Library of Congress, reproduction number LC-USZ62-125142.

Hannah Allen told of a task believed constructive for small girls, free or enslaved: "After I washed the supper dishes, I would have to go upstairs and cut out quilts, and I did not like it, but it was good for me." Martha Colquitt remembered, "Our beds had big homemade posties and frames, and we used ropes for springs. Grandma … used to piece up a heap of quilts out of our old clothes and any kind of scraps she could get a hold of." Anne Bell, a small child before emancipation, also recalled the beds: "Good wheat-straw mattresses to sleep on, cotton quilts, spreads, and cotton pillows."[10]

Written memories also mention quilts in slave life. In his autobiography, L.J. Coppin, born in 1848 into slavery in Maryland, wrote that his mother "would rise early and work till late. She made the clothing for the family, knit the stockings, made and quilted the bedspreads of which there was always a plenty on hand." Plantation owner Susan Smedes's memoir framed a nostalgic landscape of plantation life, recalling the cabins of the slaves as "clean and orderly, their beds gay with bright quilts."[11]

Detail of *Star of Bethlehem Variation*, page 14.

Star of Bethlehem Variation made by Ellen Morton Littlejohn and Margaret Morton Bibb, near Russellville, Kentucky, 1837–1850. Photograph courtesy of the Metropolitan Museum of Art. Gift of Robert Morton and Dr. Paul C. Morton (62.144). All rights reserved.

This silk masterpiece with stuffed quilting was donated to the Metropolitan Museum of Art with the story that it was made by slaves. Many museums own quilts with such attributions, but few quilts are as well documented as this one. Independent researcher Claire Somersille Nolan examined the evidence in the quilt—its style, pattern, and fabric. She also used public records, written memoirs, photographs, and unpublished writings to study the plantation families—both black and white. She concluded that this quilt is indeed a slave-made quilt.[12]

Public records include testimony presented to the Southern Claims Commission long after the war, when people could request pensions and redress from the federal government for possessions lost to Union soldiers. Nancy Johnson, once a slave on a Georgia plantation, complained that while she tried to hide her things from the invading Yankees, "They found our meat, it was hidden under the house, and they took a crop of rice [and] two fine bedquilts. They took them out. These were all my own labor and night labor." This implies that she made the quilts at night on what little of her own time she was permitted.[13]

There are also records, written at the time or narrated 80 years later in WPA interviews, of slaves making quilts for their masters' use. During the Civil War, slaveholder Kate Stone wrote, "Mamma had several of the women from the quarter sewing. Nothing to be done in the fields—too muddy. They put in and finished quilting a comfort." Later in the month, she wrote, "Mamma has finished the silk quilt, octagons of blue and yellow satin … She has had several comforts made during the bad weather."[14]

Chintz quilt made by members of the Jones family at Montevideo plantation in Liberty County, Georgia, about 1855. 92″ × 91″. Photograph courtesy of the Kenan Research Center at the Atlanta History Center.

This high-style chintz quilt, which looks to date from 1840 to 1860, is attributed to a member of the Charles Colcock Jones family, well-to-do slaveholders whose correspondence has been published in the Pulitzer Prize–winning book *The Children of Pride*. Charles's wife, Mary, often mentioned quilts in her letters. In 1862, she referred to a chintz spread on her bed, which may be this quilt. A second book of Jones family correspondence has been published in which Mary also writes of quilts. In 1850, Mary informed her sons, students at Princeton, that their "aunt still continues very feeble. Last week she quilted her laid-work [appliqué] quilt at Mrs. Winn's." In 1852, Mary wrote her niece, Laura, that she was in Philadelphia, shopping for chintz: "I will try to find the birds and butterflies for [Betsy's] quilt."[15]

We cannot know which family members had a hand in this particular quilt. There is a real possibility, as with any American quilt passed down in a family that held slaves, that enslaved women made part or all of it. On the one hand, documented slave-made quilts are rare; on the other, quilts made by slaves are quite common. The problem is finding evidence of the seamstress' identity.

In 1861, Georgia slave owner Mary Jones wrote a note to her daughter: "Tell my dear little granddaughter Grandma sends a little quilt for her bed … perhaps you could make Lucy quilt it." Careful reading of these entries reveals that the white women were not actually doing the quilting but rather were "having" the quilts and comforters made or "making" a slave do the work, a task that a number of former slaves also remembered. Fannie Moore told how her mother "worked in the field all day and pieced and quilted all night. [I had] to hold the light for her to see by." She also remembered helping her mother tack or tie quilts.[16]

With all the evidence, we can safely assume that slaves made quilts. By comparing surviving documented examples with the great number of mainstream quilts, we can assume that quilts stitched by women in slavery looked much like those done by neighboring white women.

Time and region were more important to quilt design than race or condition of servitude. Women living in the tidewater areas of Virginia or Maryland were likely to use imported chintzes; women living in the border states might stitch bright appliqués with Pennsylvania-German inspired patterns; and women in the backwoods, where home weaving remained an occupation, might make coarse "linsey" quilts of wool and cotton combination fabrics. The distinguishing factor of slave-made quilts might be between those made for their owners and those made to warm their own families.

CHAPTER 3

Samplers and Quilts Recalling Slavery Days

Getting Started

The blocks that follow tell the story of American slavery. Each was chosen for its name—to symbolize a chapter in the tale told in chronological order from capture in Africa to Reconstruction after the Civil War.

You'll find many options for using these blocks in sampler quilts or as repeat-block designs. Experienced quilters will want to begin stitching with the first block. Note that each block is marked with a difficulty level. The first one, Chained Star, is among the more difficult because it has Y seams that require some skill to piece.

If you are new to quilts, you'll want to begin with a beginner pattern, like The Second Block: Lost Ship (page 33) or The Seventeenth Block: Beauregard Surrounded (page 86). On page 103, you'll find a lesson plan for a patchwork project you can do with kids, teaching history and quiltmaking at the same time.

Choose a color palette that suits your taste and decorating style. The quilts pictured offer a variety of color ideas—some reflecting the homespun look that characterized the clothing of slavery, others pieced of reproduction prints to echo the nineteenth century. Several are made with modern fabric styles, giving traditional design a brand new look. A few have been made in ethnic fabrics—prints from Africa, New Zealand, or Asia—reflecting tribal dyes and designs.

In the sections on Other Setting Options, you'll find yardage estimates and instructions for arranging blocks in sets for four blocks, five blocks, or on up to twenty blocks. The quilts are somewhat modular—blocks are usually 15″ square, the sashing from 3″ to 5″, and the borders ranging from 3″ to 9″. This means variations are easy to plan and you can change your mind as you work. If you enjoy making a certain block, you can make nineteen more and set your quilt like *Follow the Drinking Gourd* (page 75).

A word about techniques

This book is designed to help beginning quilters, whether children or adults, finish a project. But it is a book about history, pattern, and design, rather than about techniques. For information on techniques and quilting suggestions for finished projects, see the following C&T books: *The Art of Classic Quiltmaking,* by Harriet Hargrave and Sharyn Craig; *Setting Solutions* and *Great Sets,* both by Sharyn Craig; *Borders, Bindings, and Edges,* by Sally Collins; *Mastering Quilt Marking,* by Pepper Cory; and *Mastering Machine Quilting,* by Harriet Hargrave. Also see *Quiltmaker's Guide to Machine Appliqué,* by Karla Menaugh and Cherié Ralston from Sunflower Co-operative.

A word about pattern measurements

Any pieced sampler offers problems in basic geometry. The blocks here are all 15″ × 15″—some based on four sections, others on three or seven. These mathematical problems are easily solved with BlockBase and Electric Quilt 5, the computer programs used to draft the patterns. The programs calculate cutting instructions when the numbers do not work out evenly. For example, dividing 15″ by 7 results in patches that should finish to 2.1429″, an absurd number when cutting cloth.

Fractions like that might work for sheet metal work—where the tolerances are in the thousandths of an inch—but the smallest standard for cutting fabric is $\frac{1}{8}$″. Therefore, the cutting directions here are rounded to the closest $\frac{1}{8}$″. One-seventh of a 15″ block should finish to $2\frac{1}{8}$″. When you multiply $2\frac{1}{8}$″ by 7, the block finishes to $14\frac{7}{8}$″—if you cut and sew it precisely. Do *not* worry about this. You can easily adjust for the $\frac{1}{16}$″ difference on either side as you piece the block to the sashing or to the next block.

Checkedy Cloth Sampler

Checkedy Cloth Sampler designed by Barbara Brackman, pieced by Pamela Mayfield, Lawrence, Kansas, 2004. Machine quilted by Rosie Mayhew. 85˝ × 105˝.

Twenty blocks of checks and stripes give a homespun look to this sampler. "Checkedy cloth" is an old Southern name for checked fabric. Barbara chose the colors for their symbolic nature. Red reminds us of slavery's violence and the abolitionists' passion, black is for Black History, and the natural tan is for the cotton crop that maintained the slave economy. Sashing frames the blocks with no additional border.

Quilt size: 85˝ × 105˝

Block size: 20 finished blocks, each 15˝

Sashing width: 5˝ finished

You Need

20 sampler blocks, finishing to 15˝

49 sashing strips

30 cornerstones

Fabric Requirements

Each block is based on a palette of dark, medium, and light color. You can buy ¼-yard pieces as indicated. If you prefer a more coordinated look, buy ¾-yard pieces of woven or printed stripes and plaids.

DARK

6 fat quarters or two ¾-yard pieces

3¼ yards for sashing

MEDIUM

9 fat quarters or three ¾-yard pieces

1 yard for cornerstones

LIGHT

9 fat quarters or three ¾-yard pieces

BACKING

7¾ yards, pieced together as shown

BATTING

Queen size (90˝ × 108˝)

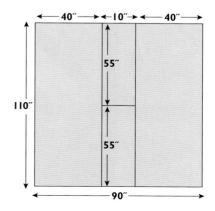

BINDING

¾ yard of dark

Cutting

CUTTING THE BLOCKS

See the cutting instructions with the individual blocks that follow.

CUTTING THE SASHING AND CORNERSTONES

Cut 49 dark rectangles 5½″ × 15½″.

Cut 30 medium squares 5½″ × 5½″.

Sewing

Diagrams showing how to sew each block are included with the individual blocks that follow.

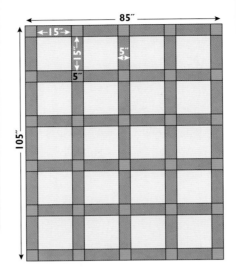

Setting the Blocks

Make 5 strips of 4 blocks and 5 sashing strips each.

Make 6 strips of 4 sashing strips and 5 cornerstones each.

Stitch the rows together, pinning carefully to be sure the cornerstones line up with the sashing grid.

Press. Quilt and bind.

Underground Railroad by Barbara Fife, Overland Park, Kansas. Machine quilted by Freda Smith. 75″ × 93″.

Barb Fife is a history buff who enjoys making quilts with historical significance. Her color scheme and fabric choices add an air of Americana to this sampler, which uses 3″ strips to sash the blocks. She embroidered the quilt's name and date by machine.

Throughout the book, you'll find quilts made with 15″ blocks in a variety of sets. Listed below are the measurements and required yardage for some. Other sets will be described in the individual projects.

Four Blocks With Sashing

My African Trip by Barbara Brackman, Lawrence, Kansas, 2005. Machine quilted by Jeanne Zyck. 39″ × 39″.

For a wall quilt using the Trip Around the World block, Barbara combined ethnic fabrics in a vivid palette of primary colors. See other examples of this set on pages 79 and 80.

Quilt size: 39″ × 39″

Block size: 15″

Sashing and border width: 3″ finished

You Need

4 blocks, finishing to 15″

12 sashing strips

9 cornerstones

Fabric Requirements

SASHING

⅔ yard dark

¼ yard bright

BACKING

1¼ yards (The backing needn't be pieced.)

BATTING

Crib size (45″ × 60″)

BINDING

½ yard

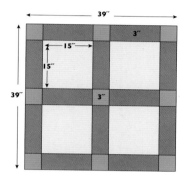

Cutting

CUTTING THE BLOCKS

See The Fourteenth Block: Trip Around the World (pages 78–80) for block cutting and sewing instructions, or choose four of your favorite blocks in the pages that follow and set them in this simple fashion.

CUTTING THE SASHING AND CORNERSTONES

Cut 12 dark rectangles 3½″ × 15½″.

Cut 9 bright square cornerstones 3½″ × 3½″.

Setting the Blocks

Make 2 strips of 2 blocks set into sashing rectangles.

Make 3 sashing strips of 2 rectangles and the cornerstones.

Join the strips.

Quilt and bind.

Five Blocks

Railroad Crossing by Carol Kirchhoff and the staff at Prairie Point Quilt Shop, Shawnee, Kansas, 2005. Machine quilted by Sandy Gore. 52″ × 52″.

When teaching a class at Carol Kirchhoff's Prairie Point Quilt Shop, Barbara developed monthly patterns that later evolved into this book. The group chose black and red to represent Black History and slavery's violence. Carol selected five of her favorite model blocks and sashed them on-point in this Railroad Crossing set.

Quilt size: 54″ × 54″

Sashing width: 2″

Border width: 3″

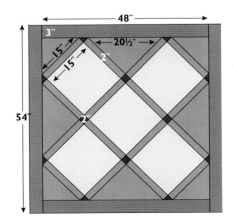

You Need

5 blocks, finishing to 15″

16 sashing strips, finishing to 2″ wide

4 square cornerstones, finishing to 2″ × 2″, plus 8 half cornerstones

4 side triangles

4 corner triangles

4 border strips, finishing to 3″ wide

Fabric Requirements

CORNERSTONES

¼ yard solid black

SASHING AND SETTING TRIANGLES

1½ yards black print

BORDER

1⅔ yards red stripe

BACKING

2½ yards, pieced as shown

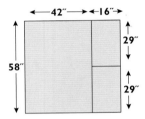

BATTING

Twin size (72″ × 90″)

BINDING

¼ yard

Cutting

CUTTING THE BLOCKS

See the appropriate blocks in the pages that follow for instructions on cutting and sewing.

CUTTING THE SASHING

Cut 16 strips 2½″ × 15½″ of black print.

CUTTING THE CORNERSTONES

Cut 4 squares 2½″ × 2½″ of black solid.

For the half triangles along the edge, cut 4 squares 2⅞″ × 2⅞″. Cut each square on the diagonal into 2 triangles. You need 8 triangles.

CUTTING THE EDGE TRIANGLES

Cut 1 square 22½″ × 22½″. Cut it on both diagonals into 4 triangles for the side triangles.

Cut 2 squares 11½″ × 11½″. Cut each square on the diagonal into 2 triangles. You need 4 corner triangles.

CUTTING THE BORDER

Cut 2 strips 3½″ × 54½″ for the sides.

Cut 2 strips 3½″ × 48½″ for the top and bottom.

Setting the Quilt

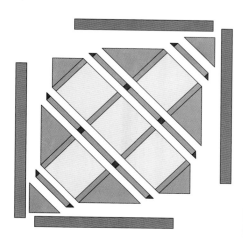

Join the blocks, sashing strips, and cornerstones into diagonal strips, as shown.

Join the strips.

Add the top and bottom borders.

Add the side borders.

Quilt and bind.

Twelve Blocks

Sampler by Gloria A. Clark, Kansas City, Kansas, 2005. 70″ × 87″.

Gloria chose twelve of the simpler blocks for a sampler that would be a good block-of-the-month set for teachers and shops. In her version, she used scraps of ethnic fabrics from home sewing projects. The challenge was coordinating the dramatic prints and bright colors. Her solution adds African textile traditions—boldly patterned prints—to contemporary color ideas. Her use of a dark, narrow spacer border to frame the blocks and pull them together visually is a popular design idea today.

This design challenge distracted Gloria while she was waiting to hear when her son would be deployed to the war in Iraq. Wars, unfortunately, come and go, and women throughout history rely on their needlework to deal with their worries.

The instructions are for the quilt in the diagram which has proportions slightly different from those Gloria used.

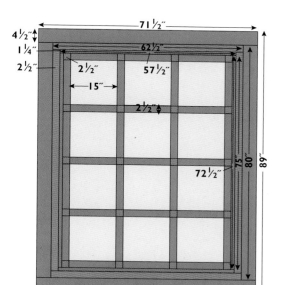

Quilt size: 71½″ × 89″

Block size: 15″

Sashing and cornerstone width: 2½″

Border width: 3 borders, finishing to 8¼″

You Need

12 blocks, finishing to 15″

20 cornerstones, finishing to 2½″ × 2½″

31 sashing strips, finishing to 15″ × 2½″

1¼″ finished inner border

2½″ finished middle border

4½″ finished outer border

Fabric Requirements

SASHING

1⅓ yards ethnic print

CORNERSTONES

¼ yard dark (or cut from inner border fabric)

BORDERS

Inner border: 2⅛ yards dark solid

Middle border: 2¼ yards bright solid

Outer border: 2¼ yards ethnic print

BACKING

5¼ yards

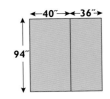

BATTING

Full/double size (81″ × 96″)

BINDING

¾ yard

Cutting

CUTTING THE BLOCKS

Gloria chose twelve of the beginner and medium blocks from the pages that follow. See cutting and sewing instructions for each block.

CUTTING THE SASHING AND CORNERSTONES

Cut 31 rectangles 15½″ × 3″ of the ethnic print.

Cut 20 squares 3″ × 3″ of the dark solid.

CUTTING THE BORDERS

Inner border (dark solid)

Cut 2 strips 1¾″ × 73″ for the sides.

Cut 2 strips 1¾″ × 58″ for the top and bottom.

Middle border (bright solid)

Cut 2 strips 3″ × 75½″ for the sides.

Cut 2 strips 3″ × 63″ for the top and bottom.

Outer border (ethnic print)

Cut 2 strips 5″ × 80½″ for the sides.

Cut 2 strips 5″ × 72″ for the top and bottom.

Setting the Quilt

Make 4 strips of 3 blocks set into sashing rectangles.

Make 5 sashing strips of 3 rectangles and 4 cornerstones.

Join the strips to make the body of the quilt.

Add the borders one at a time, stitching the side borders first, then the top and bottom borders.

Quilt and bind.

project
Star Sampler

Sweet Chariot by Jean A. Wells, Kansas City, Missouri. Machine quilted by Jeanne Zyck, 2005. 90½″ × 90½″.

Jean's star-set sampler for eight blocks contrasts the elegance of an appliquéd center with the homespun look of plaids in the pieced blocks and set. The center block, with its Union shield, is drawn from a Civil War-era sampler. Quilters who love appliqué and a setting challenge will enjoy making this quilt, which reflects classic Americana.

Quilt size: 90½" × 90½"

Block size: 15"

Border width: 9" finished

You Need

8 pieced blocks, finishing to 15"

1 center appliquéd octagon

9" finished border

Fabric Requirements

Center octagon (piece A): ⅔ yard light (Jean pieced hers of 4 light scraps.)

For appliqué: small pieces of red, white, blue, green, yellow and assorted reds.

Border: 2⅔ yards dark (Jean pieced hers of scraps.)

Triangles (piece B): 8 squares approximately 12" × 12", each of different dark plaids, or 1 yard of a single dark fabric

Trapezoids (piece C): 8 pieces ⅓ yard each of different light plaids or 2¾ yards of a single light plaid

Backing: 6⅝ yards, pieced as shown

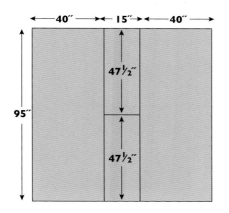

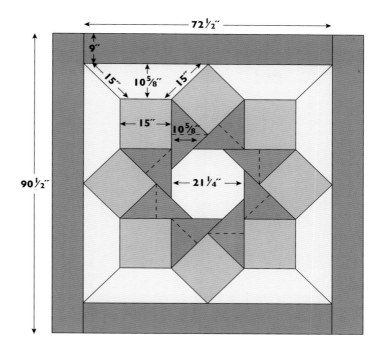

Batting: king size (120" × 120")

Binding: ¾ yard

Cutting

CUTTING THE BLOCKS

See the individual blocks that follow for cutting and sewing instructions for pieced blocks. For the central appliqué pattern, see instructions and templates on pages 25–27.

A: For the center octagon, cut a square 21¾" × 21¾". Trim 45° angles as shown 6⅛" away from each corner of the square. See pages 25–27 for appliqué cutting instructions.

CUTTING THE SETTING PIECES

B: Cut 8 squares 11½" × 11½" of various dark plaids. Cut each on the diagonal into 2 triangles. You need 16 triangles to make a set like Jean's.

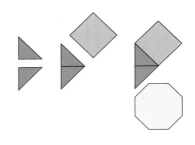

Note that Jean's border is pieced of scraps of different lengths. If you plan to use this border style, join your scraps into 9½" strips.

For the top and bottom borders, cut 2 strips 9½" × 73".

For the sides, cut 2 strips 9½" × 91".

Setting the Quilt

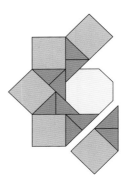

Jacob's Ladder, miniature by Ilyse Moore, hand quilted by Ilyse, Overland Park, Kansas, 2005. 36½" × 36½".

Note the star-shaped buttons in the center of this miniature masterpiece. Ilyse reduced the block size by redrafting the pieced blocks to finish 6" × 6" square and shrinking the appliqué about 50% to fit into an 8½" octagon. The border and the North Star blocks are 4" wide. This is the perfect project for computer programs BlockBase and Electric Quilt 5, which can print the classic blocks in any size.

Alternate Look— Star of a Single Fabric

If you're using a single fabric for the star, you need only cut 8 triangles by cutting 4 squares 15⅞" × 15⅞" and cutting each on the diagonal into 2 triangles. You need 8 of these larger triangles.

C: Cut 11⅛"-wide strips from the width of the light plaid fabric. From those strips, cut at 45° angles into rhomboidal shapes that measure 37⅛" on the long side and 15½" on the short.

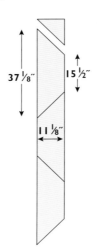

37⅛"   15½"

11⅛"

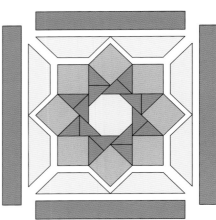

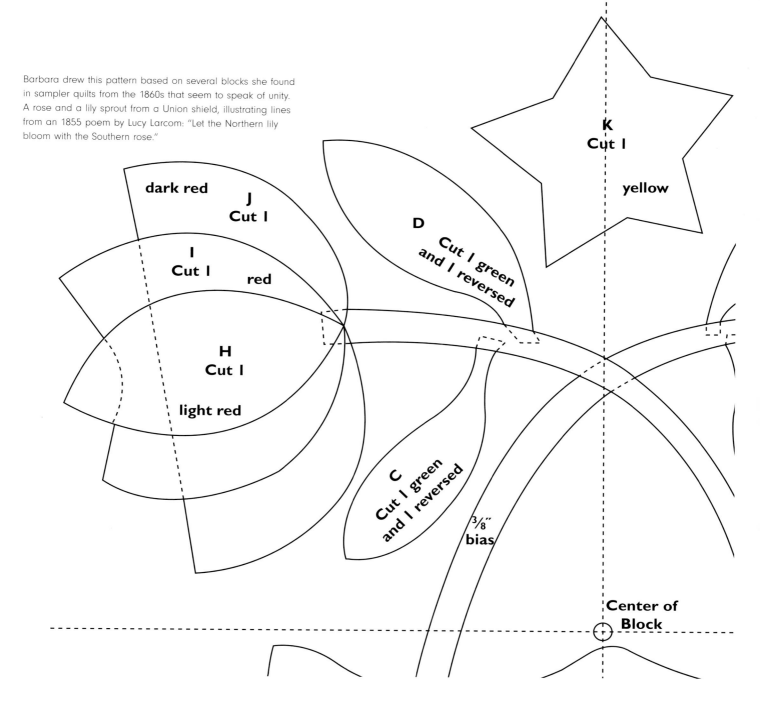

Barbara drew this pattern based on several blocks she found in sampler quilts from the 1860s that seem to speak of unity. A rose and a lily sprout from a Union shield, illustrating lines from an 1855 poem by Lucy Larcom: "Let the Northern lily bloom with the Southern rose."

K
Cut I

yellow

dark red

J
Cut I

I
Cut I

red

D
Cut I green and I reversed

H
Cut I

light red

C
Cut I green and I reversed

3/8"
bias

Center of Block

Piece the stripes for the shield by cutting 5″-long 1½″ strips. Alternate four red stripes and three white ones into a rectangle 7½″ × 5″ and cut the shield. Or save time by finding a patriotic striped fabric and cut the shield from that.

If you are piecing your setting triangles of plaids, as Jean did, combine 2 smaller pieces to make 8 larger triangles.

Stitch each block to a setting triangle.

Piece the first pair to the octagon, seaming just a part of the triangle and leaving the rest of the seam free for now.

Add the blocks as you go around the octagon counterclockwise.

Finish the final seam to create the star.

Join each trapezoid to a block.

Join the mitered corners.

BORDERS
Add the top and bottom borders first.

Finish with the side borders.

Quilt and bind.

CHAPTER 4

The Blocks

Most of the blocks are shaded in dark, medium, and light fabric, with perhaps a darker medium and a lighter medium for a total of four or five shades. One fat quarter of each fabric (measuring 18″ × 22″) will give you more than enough fabric for each block.

Jacob's Ladder Sampler Quilt by the Northwest Arkansas Quilt Study Group, Rogers, Arkansas. Machine quilted by Karen Kielmeyer, 2005. 85″ × 102½″.

Members of the group—Susan Burghart, Christine Clardy, Jo Ann Collier, Charlotte Enfield, Rheba Ford, Linda Hancock, Charlotte Hannan, Edith Idleman, Dorothy LeBoeuf, Paula Mariedaughter, Mary Pumphrey, Ardith Winters, and Nora Cope—combined ethnic prints with reproduction fabrics that echo the years before the Civil War into a wonderfully integrated composition.

Chained Star

A Block to Recall Capture in Africa

Chained Star by Dorothy LeBoeuf, Rogers, Arkansas.

A daguerreotype taken in the 1850s of Mollie, in the service of the John and Eliza Partridge family in Monticello, Florida. Mollie, born in Africa, was the children's nurse. One of her charges recalled the white children enjoyed visiting Mollie's cabin, where she fed them a "homely meal of fried bacon and ash cake [bread cooked in the hot ashes of the stove]." Photograph courtesy of the State Library and Archives of Florida.

15″ Block

Level of difficulty: Skilled

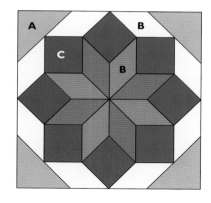

Cutting

A: Cut 2 medium squares 5¼″ × 5¼″. Cut each on the diagonal to make 2 triangles. You need 4 light triangles.

B: Cut 2⅞″-wide strips. Use the template to cut 45° angles. Cut 8 bright or red diamonds for the star. Cut 8 light diamonds for the chain.

C: Cut 8 dark squares 3⅝″ × 3⅝″.

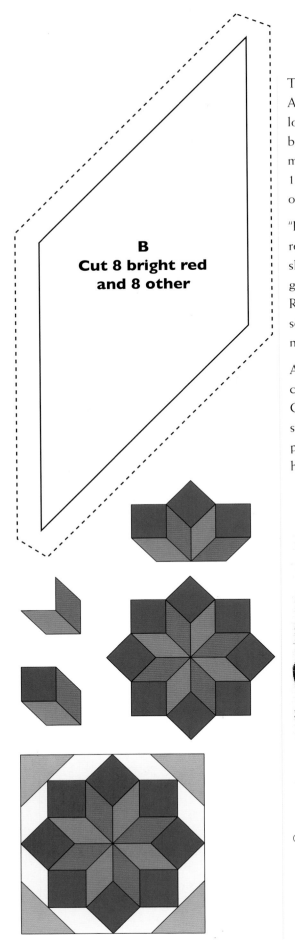

B
**Cut 8 bright red
and 8 other**

The chain of written tradition is difficult to trace back to life in Africa. After the United States outlawed slave ships in 1807, traders could no longer transport captured Africans. Most nineteenth-century slaves were born in the United States, so few written words recall a life before enslavement. One memory was recorded, second-hand, in a New Jersey diary in 1810. The enslaved woman, whose name is not known, often told her owner of her capture during a battle:

"I love to get her talking about Guinea, and she loves it too. She can only remember that the people were all fighting and the town was on fire when she was carried away. One black man she will never forget. He tore all her gold ornaments from her, and when she cried, boxed her ears. 'Miss Rachel,' she will say, 'I never will forgive that man. Great ugly fellow! If I see him on the day of Judgment, I'll know him. I'll mark him down—I'll never forget him.'"[17]

An oral history recorded during the WPA project gave another view of capture, one in which the family bears responsibility. Former slave Peter Corn told the interviewer a tale he may have heard in his youth: "The first starting of slavery was when a white man would go over to Africa and the people there were ignorant and the white man would hold up a pretty red handkerchief and trade it for one of the Negro woman's children."[18]

Captives en route to a slave ship, from a nineteenth-century book.

Other stories tell of young women trapped by slavers who used bright red cloth for bait. Fabric hanging from a tree or strewn on the ground might cause a girl to stray from the road into the arms of her kidnappers, according to a story told by Richard Jones in a WPA interview. He was, by his calculations, 125 years old when he recalled how his grandmother was enticed aboard a ship:

"Well do I remember my Granny from Africa, and straight from there too … Granny Judith said that in Africa they had very few pretty things and that they had no red colors in cloth. In fact, they had no cloth at all. Some strangers with pale faces came one day and dropped a small piece of red flannel down on the ground. All the black folks grabbed for it. Then a larger piece was dropped a little further on … They just dropped red flannel to them like we drop corn to chickens to get them on the roost at night."[19]

The pattern Chained Star is a traditional design that was published in Ruth Finley's 1929 book *Old Patchwork Quilts and the Women Who Made Them*. Finley collected a bit of folklore with patterns she found in Ohio, New York, and Connecticut. She mentioned no symbolism for this nineteenth-century star, but our poetic license allows us to view the chains linking the background as metaphors for the frightening stories of kidnapping. The star might be red to stand for both the heart of the captive and the red cloth that caught her eye.

Star of Africa

Star of Africa, pieced by Barbara Brackman, Lawrence, Kansas, 2005. Machine quilted by Pamela Mayfield. 37ʺ × 37ʺ.

Four blocks of African-style fabrics make a wallhanging or baby quilt. Prints from different cultures capture the look of natural dyes, such as indigo blues and madder browns. Several prints have the look of batik designs, which are traditionally printed with a waxy substance before the cotton is dipped in the dyebath.

Barbara isolated images in the star points by cutting a clear plastic template and lining up the pattern exactly the same for each point on the fabric. The effect is kaleidoscopic, with the center of the star creating a complex secondary design.

Quilt size: 37ʺ × 37ʺ

Block size: 15ʺ

Border width: 3½ʺ finished

You Need

4 Chained Star blocks, finishing to 15ʺ (pattern on pages 29–30)

4 border strips

1 sheet of plastic template material 7ʺ × 7ʺ

1 felt tip marker to mark the template

Fabric Requirements

This quilt grew out of the fabric. Barbara began with large-scale ethnic fabrics that she fussy cut. Look for human figures, animals, or geometrics and let those prints dictate your color scheme. Barbara wanted to echo the natural dyes that have been used around the world for centuries. Once she found the large prints, she chose coordinating blues and browns.

BLOCKS

½ yard each of 4 large-scale ethnic prints

You need at least ½ yard of the large-scale prints to form the stars, but check your fabric to make sure you have 8 exact repeats in each piece. If not, buy a larger piece. The fussy cutting is quite wasteful of fabric. Your leftovers will look like Swiss cheese when you're finished, but the effect is worth it.

4 fat quarters dark brown

4 fat quarters light brown

2 fat quarters dark blue

2 fat quarters light blue

BORDERS

1¼ yards dark blue print

BACKING

1¼ yards

BATTING

Crib size (45″ × 60″)

BINDING

⅓ yard dark blue

Cutting

CUTTING THE BLOCKS

Cut a clear plastic template the size of template B (page 30).

Choose the figure in the large print that will repeat. Place the plastic template so it is centered on top of this figure. Mark the outline of the figure with a felt tip pen.

Trace around the diamond template onto the fabric.

Move the template to another repeat, line it up exactly, and mark the fabric. Repeat this 8 times. If you can't find 8 repeats, 2 sets of 4 will do. Note the block in the upper right repeats the head of the snake alternating with the tail.

Cut out the pieces.

CUTTING THE BORDERS

Cut 2 strips 4″ × 30½″ for the top and bottom borders.

Cut 2 strips 4″ × 37½″ for the sides.

Setting the Quilt

Piece the blocks together.

Add the top and bottom borders.

Add the side borders.

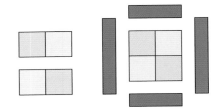

" I hear them tell that my grandparents came from Africa. They fooled them to come or I call it fooling them. [At the] dock, they blew a whistle and the people came from all over the country to see what it was. They fooled them on the vessel and give them something to eat. Shut them up and don't let them get out. Some of them jump over board and try to get home, but they couldn't swim and go down. Lots of them still lost down there in the sea, or I reckon they're still down there because they ain't got back yet. "

—Charlie Grant, recalling family stories for a WPA interviewer, 1937[20]

Lost Ship
A Block to Recall the Ocean Voyage

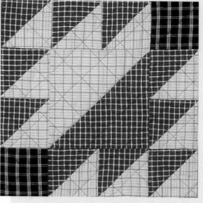

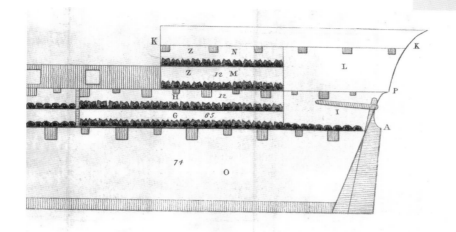

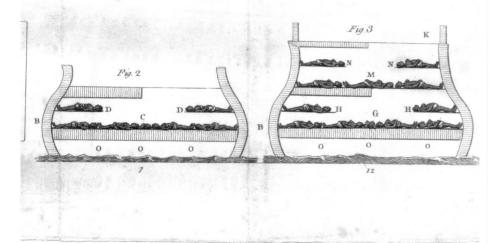

A plan for packing a deck with human beings was first published in 1788.[21]

Lost Ship by Pamela Mayfield, Lawrence, Kansas.

15″ Block

Level of difficulty: Beginner

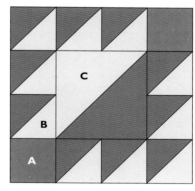

Cutting

A: Cut 2 medium squares 4¼″ × 4¼″.

B: Cut 5 dark and 5 light squares 4⅝″ × 4⅝″. Cut each square on the diagonal to make 10 dark and 10 light triangles.

C: Cut 1 light and 1 dark square 8⅜″ × 8⅜″. Cut each on the diagonal to make 1 dark and 1 light triangle. (You only need one of each triangle.)

Prime among terrible stories of slavery were tales of the ships carrying Africans to the New World. Clippers set out on the ocean, and the crew was callous about the safety of their human cargo. Only three of every four people packed into the holds arrived alive in the Americas.

The 1997 film *Amistad*, starring Morgan Freeman, depicts the true story of a ship smuggling slaves in 1839, more than 30 years after importation was declared illegal. By that time, slavery had been abolished in the British Empire and in many American countries except the United States, which continued to defend its slave economy against world criticism.

This Lost Ship pattern is adapted from an old design to show a slave ship and a lost ship in a single block. We can add more symbolism to our sampler by viewing the three triangles on the side as the ghosts of the three of every four captives who survived the awful ocean voyage—survivors who may have envied the dead.

Lost Ships by Lavon E. Wynn, Kansas City, Kansas, 2005. 37½″ × 37½″.

Lavon featured an African print by piecing four blocks in the traditional Lost Ship design, an old pattern that makes good use of high-contrast shading. The Ladies' Art Company of St. Louis, which began selling patterns about 1890, included this design in their mail order catalog. When blocks are set side by side, a ghost ship appears behind the darker ships.

THE THIRD BLOCK

Cotton Boll

A Block to Recall the Slave Economy

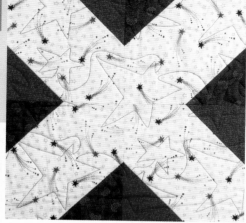

Cotton Boll by Barbara Fife, Overland Park, Kansas.

Men continue the traditional hard labor of picking cotton in this postcard photograph, about 1910.

15″ Block

Level of difficulty: Beginner

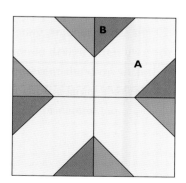

Cutting

A: Cut 2 strips 5¾″ wide. Use the template to cut the angles. Cut 4 light (cotton-colored) shapes.

B: Cut 2 dark and 2 medium squares 4⅝″ × 4⅝″. Cut each on the diagonal to make 2 triangles. You need 4 dark and 4 medium triangles.

  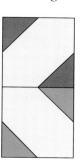 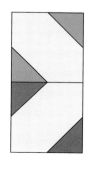

Cabin Windows
A Block to Recall Plantation Housing

Cabin Windows (variation) by Dorothy LeBoeuf, Rogers, Arkansas.

Artelia Bendolph of Gees Bend, Alabama was photographed by Arthur Rothstein in 1937. The cabin windows with shutters or slip doors had not changed in this community. Photo courtesy of the Library of Congress, reproduction number LC-USF 34-025359-D.

15″ Block

Level of difficulty: Moderate

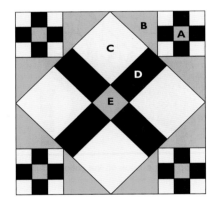

Cutting

A: Cut 16 light, 4 medium, and 16 dark squares $1\frac{3}{4}″ \times 1\frac{3}{4}″$.

B: Cut 4 medium squares $4\frac{5}{8}″ \times 4\frac{5}{8}″$. Cut each on the diagonal to make 2 triangles. You need 8 triangles.

C: Cut 4 light squares $4\frac{7}{8}″ \times 4\frac{7}{8}″$.

D: Cut 4 dark rectangles $2\frac{1}{4}″ \times 4\frac{7}{8}″$.

E: Cut 1 medium square $2\frac{1}{4}″ \times 2\frac{1}{4}″$.

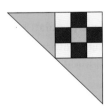

We have many historic resources for viewing nineteenth-century plantation life, including accounts of Northern travelers and Europeans, diaries and letters of plantation owners, and books written by escaped slaves. When writers in the government's WPA project talked to former slaves in the 1930s, they used standardized interview questions, so we find many consistencies across the interviews, especially in descriptions of clothing and housing.

Missourian Betty Abernathy remembered, "The white folk had a nice big house and there were a number of poor little cabins for us folks. Ours was one room, built of logs, and had a puncheon [rough log] floor." Annie Bridges, born eight years before the Emancipation Proclamation, said, "We lived in a log cabin with two rooms. Yes, there was a floor and we had a bed, but it hadn't any mattress, just roped and corded. Holes were cut in the side of the bed, so the ropes could go through."[25]

An engraving from an 1856 book, *Slavery Unmasked,* contrasts work and play on the plantation.

Frederick Ross, who'd been a Missouri slave, recalled, "Our cabin was just one room with a big fireplace at one end. There was always a big kettle hanging in the chimney and one of those iron ovens sitting on the hearth. There were five in our family and we had one big bed and a trundle bed that would roll under the other bed, like that. Feather beds? Whew. We had the biggest feather beds. You should have seen the big flock of geese we had."[26]

Many people remarked about the cabin windows. Tourist Frederica Bremer painted a sunny picture of slave life for her Swedish readers: "The slave villages … have rather a comfortable appearance, excepting that one very rarely sees glass in the windows of their houses. The window generally consists of a square opening, which is closed with a shutter. But so also are those in the houses of the poor white people."[27]

W. C. Parson Allen told a WPA interviewer: "We lived in log cabins. They had slip doors on the windows. Man, what you talking about? We never saw a window glass. Had about fourteen cabins and they were placed so that the old master could sit on his porch and see every one of them." A slip door might be a sliding wooden door, represented by the pattern Cabin Windows. The quilt design is not common, although it is made up of common nine-patches, which are easy enough for a beginner.[28]

" My first recollections are of Mammy. I remember the little stool in her cabin that was kept for my use … I can still see the walls in her cabin festooned with strings of red pepper, bachelor buttons, and ropes of chips of yellow pumpkin. Her small looking glass was encircled with cedar twigs that had been dipped in flour. "

—Rebecca Latimer Felton, 1919[29]

Slave Chain (variation) by Jean A. Wells,
Kansas City, Missouri.

THE FIFTH BLOCK

Slave Chain
A Block to Recall the Slave's Clothing

Union army photographer James Gibson recorded refugees at Foller's House
in Cumberland Landing, Virginia, on May 14, 1862. Photograph courtesy of the
Library of Congress (reproduction number LC-B8171-0383).

15˝ Block

Level of difficulty: Skilled

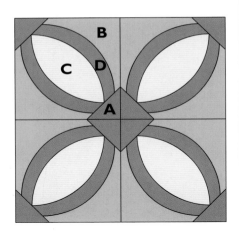

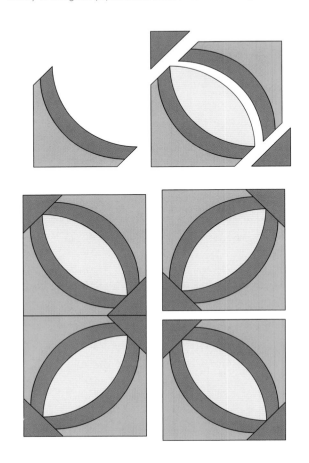

Cutting

A: Rotary cut 4 dark squares $3\frac{3}{8}˝ \times 3\frac{3}{8}˝$.
Cut each on the diagonal to make to
make 2 triangles. You need 8.

B, C, D: Use the templates to cut the
pieces indicated.

Slave Chain, designed by Barbara Brackman, pieced and appliquéd by Jean Stanclift, Lawrence, Kansas. Machine quilted by Charlotte Gurwell, 2001. 76" × 76".

Chains were a degrading symbol of slavery. To prevent escape, slaves on the move were often chained together in a line called a *coffle*. Abraham Lincoln recalled an 1841 river trip to St. Louis when he wrote a friend: "You may remember, as I well do, that … there were on board, ten or a dozen slaves, shackled together with irons. That sight was a continual torment to me and I see something like it every time I touch the Ohio, or any other slave border."[30]

Slaves were also identified by their clothing, marking them as surely as a leg iron. Frederick Olmstead, traveling in the antebellum South on a Sunday morning, noticed African-Americans going to church wearing "clothing of coarse gray 'negro cloth,' that appeared as if made by contract, without regard to the size of the particular individual to whom it had been allotted, like penitentiary uniforms. A few had a better suit of coarse blue cloth, expressly made for them, evidently, for 'Sunday clothes.'" Tourist Harriett Martineau wrote of Alabama "black women ploughing in the field, with their ugly, scanty, dingy dresses."[31]

Long after emancipation, Georgia Baker told a WPA interviewer about her clothing: "Dresses made of yarn cloth … and petticoats and drawers made out of osnaburg. Children that were big enough done the spinning, and Aunt Betsey and Aunt Finny, they wove most every night till they rung the bell at ten o'clock for us to go to bed. We made bolts and bolts of cloth every year. We went barefoot in summer, but bless your sweet life we had good shoes in winter and wore good stockings, too. It took three shoemakers for our plantation. They made up holestock shoes for the women and gals and brass-toed brogans for the men and boys."[32]

Holestock shoes, she explained, were sturdy shoes with "extra pieces on the sides so we wouldn't knock holes in them too quick." A woman identified as Aunt Sarah talked about brogan shoes, which women wore as well as men: "Don't you know what they looked like? They was neither lined or bound, and we used a pegging awl to make holes for the laces. Some of them had copper toes."[33]

Osnaburg was a coarse cloth, factory woven in New England and Germany or on the plantations. George and Martha Washington's records include a 1759 order for 450 Ells (yards) of "Oznaburgs" and "40 Yards of Coarse Jeans or fustians for summer frocks for Negro Servants." Willis Winn, who believed he was born in 1822, told a WPA interviewer that "slaves didn't wear nothing but white Lowell cloth. They gave us pants for Sunday that had a black stripe down the leg."

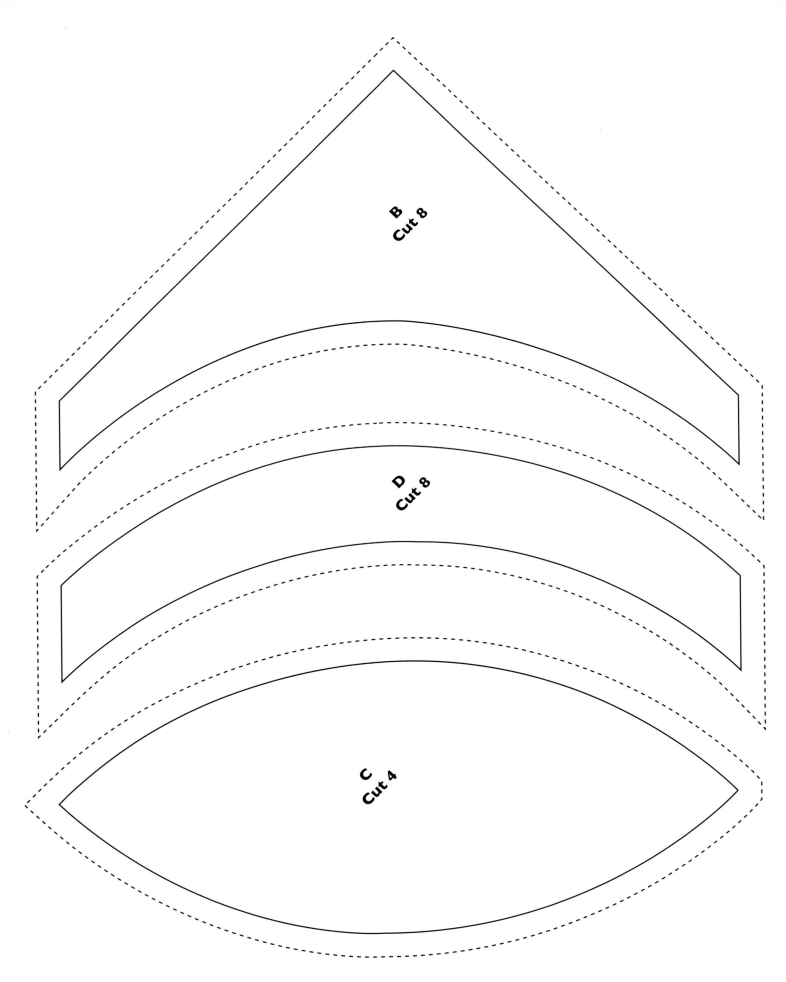

B
Cut 8

D
Cut 8

C
Cut 4

Lowell cloth was probably a coarsely woven cloth from the mills in Lowell, Massachusetts.[34]

Frederick Douglass listed in his memoir the slaves' annual clothing allowance. Men received "two tow-linen shirts, such linen as the coarsest crash towels are made of, and a pair of tow-linen trousers for summer." For winter, trousers and jacket "of woolen, most slazily put together," plus a pair of "yarn stockings," and "shoes of the coarsest description." By "slazily," Douglass means sleazily or loosely woven; tow and crash were rough linen fabrics.[35]

Children too young to work wore shifts, as described in a WPA interview by George Bollinger: "Us children never wore no pants, just something like a long shirt made of homespun." Louis Hill, who was a small child during slavery, recalled, "We generally wore a straight slip like a nightgown and it fastened round the neck … Take this off and we were naked." Boys still in shifts were called "shirt-tail boys."[36]

Sarah Graves, about ten years old when the Civil War began, remembered spinning and weaving woolen fabric in Kentucky: "We would shear the sheep, wash the wool, card it, spin it, and weave it. If we wanted it striped, we used two threads. We would color one by using herbs or barks. Sometimes we had it carded at a mill, and sometimes we carded it ourselves. But when we did it, the threads were short, which caused us to have to tie the thread often, making too many knots in the dress. I have gathered the wool off the fences where it had been caught off the sheep and washed, and used it to make mittens."[37]

Stripes and checks were common patterns in slave clothing. In 1846, slaveholder Thomas Chaplin recorded in his diary that he bought "Negro summer cloth": "I gave out the cloth … Got striped homespun. Negroes are delighted with it." His opinion contrasts with that held by some women who actually had to wear the fabric. Slave owner Grace Brown Elmore noted during clothing shortages after the Civil War that women who were once in slavery were "delighted [to] procure a dress of the striped homespun they used to hate."[38]

Women in slavery often wore a headscarf or "chignon" tied around their heads, sometimes of a bright patterned cloth. A kerchief over their shoulders and a checked apron completed the outfit. Anyone hoping to escape and blend into society as a free person needed to find suitable clothing, because their usual wardrobe branded them. One of the first steps in helping a woman escape was providing a bonnet and gloves and replacing her brogans with ladylike footwear.

Dan Josiah Lockhart emphasized clothing's importance in the story of his escape. He obtained a good suit of clothes and took passage on a ferry across the Potomac River. He met two men, one black, one white. The black man asked if he was free. "It staggered me at first to think that a colored man should ask me that question. The white man reproved him: 'What the devil do you ask that question for? Do you think a man dressed like him can be a runaway?'"[39]

Slave Chain or Job's Tears, maker unknown, about 1940. The sampler block is adapted from one pictured in Ruth Finley's 1929 book, *Old Patchwork Quilts*. Her pattern had an octagonal center like this one. She gave it six names: Job's Tears, Slave Chain, Texas Tears, Rocky Road to Kansas, Kansas Troubles, and Endless Chain. The pattern is so unusual that Barbara can't recall seeing a nineteenth-century quilt using it. This is actually the only example she has ever found.

Rough work clothing was put aside in favor of silk and calico, top hats, and frock coats. Most important was time off to work for oneself or to visit family members on other plantations. WPA interviewees remembered regional variations in the holiday, with South Carolinians, for example, describing only a day or two of rest, while Missourians remembered a week off. In some places, time off was defined by the burning of the Yule Log. When the embers died, the holiday was over. "Some took advantage and would cut their ... log as soon as Christmas was over for the next and put it in a pond of water to soak for a year," according to slaveholder Mary DeHaven, who remembered life on a Louisiana plantation.[41]

Eliza Madison told a WPA writer about a version of Santa Claus: "We'd get candy or a new dress. On one Christmas, old Christine or Santa Clause would wrap up in a blanket and this is how we got our presents. Down there the hickory nuts grew big and it was a funny thing when we found out that old Christine was giving us our own hickory nuts." Another interviewee had childhood memories of receiving "a pair of stockings and some candy and apples. For the men folks, they sometimes got whiskey." John Estell recalled the grown-up's pleasures: "At Christmas, the old boss would fix a big bowl of eggnog for us."[42]

Escaped slave Frederick Douglass noted that in Maryland, the holiday was "used or abused nearly as we pleased. Those of us who had families at a distance were generally allowed to spend the whole six days in their society." Slaves might spend the time working for themselves, making tools and baskets or hunting meat. "But by far the larger part engaged in such sports and merriments as playing ball, wrestling, running footraces, fiddling, dancing and drinking whiskey ... A slave who would work during the holidays was considered by our masters as scarcely deserving them."

Douglass recognized the method in the week of mirth. The Christmas holiday was an annual concession by the slave owners, a "most effective means ... in keeping down the spirit of insurrection ... These holidays serve as ... safety-valves, to carry off the rebellious spirit of enslaved humanity."[43]

After the Civil War, American holiday customs lost much of their regional style. People around the nation began to celebrate the New Englander's Thanksgiving, the New Yorker's New Year's Day, and the Southerner's Christmas. A few Christmas customs—firecrackers and cannon firing—mercifully have been forgotten.

Christmas Star is a pattern that is also called Georgetown Circle, Crown of Thorns, or Wedding Ring, among many other names. The *Oklahoma Farmer Stockman*, an agricultural newspaper with a quilt column for the farm wife, printed this name in about 1930. We can use it to symbolize the event—a holiday, a religious observance, and an important part of slavery's annual calendar.

"Christmas was the time of all time on that old plantation ... Every child brought a stocking up to the Big House to be filled. They all wanted one of the mistress's stockings, because now she weighed nigh on three hundred pounds."

—Prince Johnson in a WPA interview, about 1938[44]

Triple Link Chain

A Block to Recall Family Ties

Children on an eroding North Carolina farm were photographed in 1938 by Marion Post Wolcott. Almost 75 years after the Civil War poverty reigned, but there was comfort in the knowledge that families could no longer be forcibly separated. Photo courtesy of the Library of Congress, reproduction number LC-USF34-050720.

Triple Link Chain (variation) by Diane Weber, Lawrence, Kansas.

15″ Block

Level of difficulty: Skilled

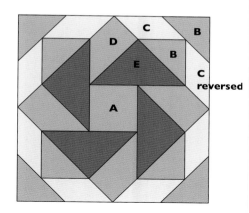

Cutting

A: Cut 1 dark square 4¼″ × 4¼″.

B: Cut 4 dark squares 4⅝″ × 4⅝″. Cut each on the diagonal to make 2 triangles. You need 8 triangles.

C: Cut light strips 2⅜″. Use the template to cut the 45° angles going one way. Flip over the template to cut 4 reversed.

D: Cut dark strips 3⅛″. Use the template to cut the 45° angle, making 4 of the shape.

E: Cut 2 medium squares 6⅛″ × 6⅛″. Cut each on the diagonal to make 2 triangles. You need 4 triangles.

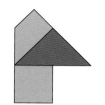

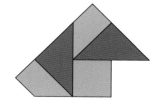

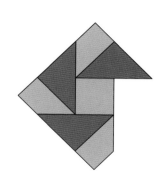

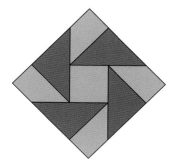

Slavery caused countless personal tragedies, but it is the instability of family life that rings the deepest chord in the heart. Slaves lived in perpetual anxiety that children would be torn away, lovers forbidden to see each other, and spouses shipped to other plantations. Family breakup is a continual theme in memoirs and first-hand accounts and is summarized in a letter Emily Nixon wrote to her mother in 1836. Thomas and Amy Nixon had been able to purchase their own freedom and free two of their seven children, but they had to leave daughter Emily behind:

"My dear Mother—In my last letter to you I felt happy to tell you all about my wedding—but, ah! Mother, what have I to tell you now? A cloud has settled upon me and produced a change in my prospect, too great for words to express. My husband is torn from me and carried away by his master ... Although he [his master] was offered $800 for him that we might not be parted, he refused it ... All my entreaties and tears did not soften his hard heart ... O! Mother, what shall I do? A time is fast approaching when I shalt want my husband and mother, and both are gone!"[45]

Emily used coded words commonly understood at the time to tell her mother she was pregnant. "A time is fast approaching" probably means she was expecting to give birth soon. Joy in childbirth was often tempered by fears that children would be sold by greedy owners. Charity Bower, born in 1782, told Lydia Maria Child her life story in 1848:

"Sixteen children I've had, first and last ... From the time my first baby was born, I always set my heart upon buying freedom for some of my children. I thought it was of more consequence to them than to me; for I was old and used to being a slave. But Mistress McKinley wouldn't let me have my children. One after another—one after another—she sold them away from me. Oh, how many times that woman broke my heart!"[46]

The sampler pattern, adapted from Triple Link Chain, published in the Nancy Cabot column of the *Chicago Tribune*, recalls three ways slaves were denied the basic human rights to emotional connections. First, children were sold away from their parents. Second, husbands and wives were separated, forced to live on separate plantations, or sold. And finally, in an inevitable abuse of power, slavery encouraged a system of rape and concubinage, in which women's sexual favors were demanded by masters and bosses. But this block can also symbolize the tightness of the family bond. Stories abound of people spending decades trying to find missing family members.

Cold World, Warm Hearts by Barbara Brackman, Lawrence, Kansas, 2005. Machine quilted by Jeanne Zyck. 57˝ × 57˝. Using today's fabrics with a hand-painted look and exercising her poetic license, Barbara created a cold and stormy world where the heart of each block reflects the redeeming warmth of family life. For measurements to create a similar set for nine of the same blocks, see pages 71–72.

A family photographed in front of a quilt, about 1900.

"Slavery days was hell. I was grown up when the war come, and I was a mother before it closed. Babies were snatched from their mother's breast and sold to speculators. Children were separated from sisters and brothers and never saw each other again ... I could tell you about it all day, but even then you couldn't guess the awfulness of it."

—Delia Garlic in a WPA interview, about 1938[47]

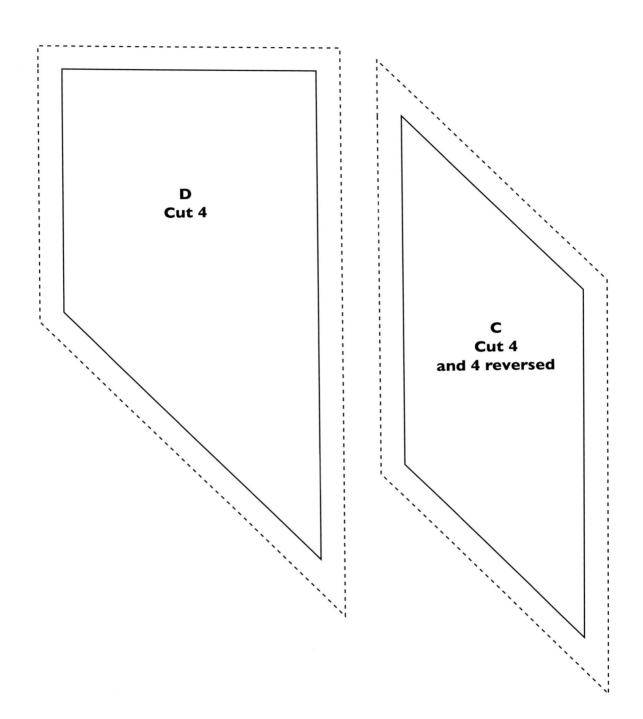

D
Cut 4

C
Cut 4
and 4 reversed

Charm

A Block to Recall African Tradition

Painter Ben Shahn was employed by the federal Farm Security Project to document poverty. His photo of an unnamed child in Little Rock, Arkansas captures the common use of newspaper as wallpaper. The custom was not only functional but also symbolically linked to African traditions, a type of charm. People liked to say that any evil spirit who might want to haunt the household would first have to read every word in the wallpaper, postponing any mischief. Photo courtesy of the Library of Congress, Digital ID: reproduction number LC-DIG-fsa-8a16140.

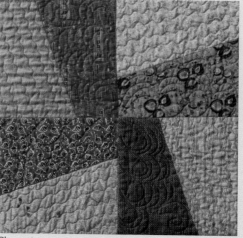

Charm (variation) by Charlotte Hannan, Rogers, Arkansas.

15″ Block

Level of difficulty: Beginner

Cutting

Cut strips 8″ wide and use template A to cut the angle. You need 2 dark, 2 medium, and 4 light strips. Remember, a true charm quilt has no two prints alike.

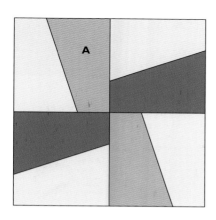

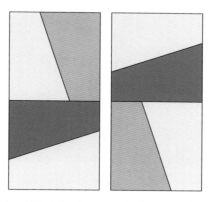

New World religion, clothing, and language tried to erase much of African memory, but to this day, African ways saturate American culture in our music, cuisine, architecture, storytelling, and countless other areas. Quiltmaking traditions, however, are hard to trace. One can point to similarities between American quilts and African textiles, but it is difficult to determine whether one culture's ideas are derived from another's, which direction the influence traveled, or whether pattern similarities are mere coincidence.

Charm quilts seem to link African and mainstream American traditions. The style, quite popular from 1870 to 1920 with quiltmakers of various ethnic origins, was described in a 1911 woman's magazine article, advising that a triangle design was "a desirable pattern for a charm-quilt, in which no two pieces are alike."[48]

Quilters cut a single pattern shape, such as a hexagon or a square, from a variety of prints. In a true charm quilt, a rather rare find, the quiltmaker never used the same print twice. One folk tradition declared a charm quilt should have 999 different pieces, with the thousandth piece the only duplicate. Another tradition promised that the first man a girl laid eyes upon after collecting the 999th print would be her future husband.[49]

The idea of charms being both variegated and magical was recorded in a WPA interview. Mollie Dawson, born a slave in Texas in 1852, remembered, "Most all the young girls had what we called a charm string." The girls asked friends and relatives for a "pretty button to put on this charm string. I have seen some of those charm strings five feet long and some of the prettiest [things] I ever saw in my life. They were a lot prettier than these beads that we buy at the store now. This charm string was supposed to bring good luck to the owner of it."[50]

After the Civil War, the term *charm string* was widely used to mean a string of variegated buttons. In 1873, the St. Louis Fair offered a premium for a charm string. A 1936 magazine article about Grandma's Charm String recalled that children collected buttons from their friends, which not only brought good luck but also served as a sort of memory book. In 1934, someone asked readers of a Springfield, Missouri, newspaper, "Do you remember the old charm strings made of strung buttons? 'Friendship strings' we called them."[51]

Flora Kennedy Cowgill, a child in Kansas about 1880, gave her insight into the rules for making a charm string. She remembered that her mother helped her string buttons from the button box into a charm string: "I showed the other girls my charm-string with pride, only to be told … that my charm-string was no good … You did not just go to your

mother's button box and string a lot of buttons." Flora's brother took advantage of the family's connection to a politician and asked him for buttons from senators and their wives, "all tagged as to whose they were. That settled the charm-string question."[52]

We can recall the durability of African customs with a Charm block. This one, a pinwheel made of an odd-shaped, four-sided patch, never seems to have been given a name in the quilt literature. It's a tessellated pattern, which means a single shape interlocks to cover the surface, with no additional pattern shapes. Hexagons, triangles, and 60° diamonds are commonly found in charm quilts.

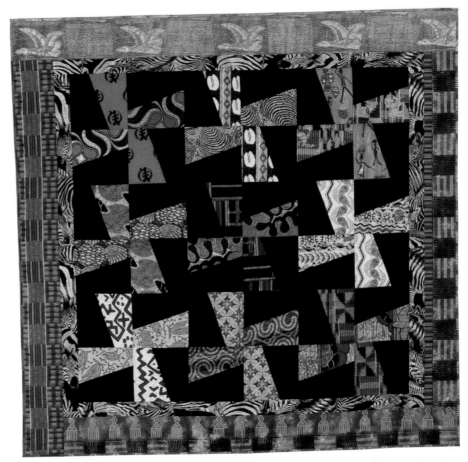

West African Charm by Dorothy LeBoeuf, Rogers, Arkansas. Machine pieced and quilted by Dorothy, 2005. 55˝ × 55˝.

Dorothy chose imported prints to echo the rich textile traditions of West Africa in this set of nine Charm blocks bordered by random strips of fabric. Her use of black for the neutral creates an effective visual puzzle.

Charm, machine pieced and quilted by Lavon E. Wynn, Kansas City, Kansas, 2005. 59″ × 59″.

Using today's bright prints, Lavon has created an eye-dazzling version of the Charm block by playing the complementary colors yellow and purple against each other. She set nine blocks side by side with three borders—a 1″ stripe, a 2″ yellow, and a 4″ purple border. Black binding frames the composition.

"

Now the gals go to the ten cent store and buy cheap perfume. In those days, they dried chinaberries and painted them and wore them on a string around their necks to charm us."

—Gus Feaster, 1937[53]

Charm quilt top, maker unknown, about 1890. Hexagons were a popular pattern for single-template charm quilts. The basket, recently purchased in Charleston, South Carolina, is coiled rather than woven, reflecting African traditions. Beads, buttons, and quilt patches are strung for decoration and storage, but none of the strings is a variegated charm string, like those described in the nineteenth century.

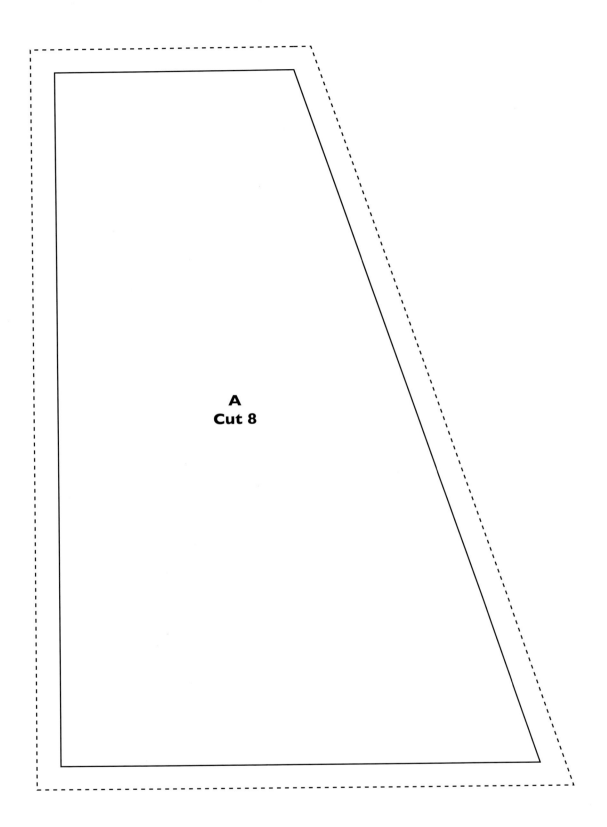

A
Cut 8

Aunt Dinah

A Block to Recall Americanization

This portrait of a musician appears to be a *carte-de-visite* photograph from about 1880. The words "Aunt Winnie" are written on the card. Winnie had been a slave in the family of Jesse Stephenson in St. Louis, Missouri. Photograph courtesy of the Library of Congress, reproduction number LC-USZ6Z-125157.

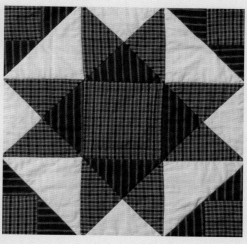

Aunt Dinah by Mary Lou Pick, Lee's Summit, Missouri.

15″ Block

Level of difficulty: Beginner

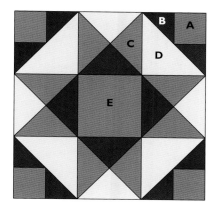

Cutting

A: Cut 4 medium squares 3″ × 3″.

B: Cut 4 dark squares 3⅜″ × 3⅜″. Cut each on the diagonal to make 2 triangles.

C: Cut 2 medium, 1 light, and 1 dark square 6¼″ × 6¼″. Cut each twice on the diagonals to make 4 triangles. You need 8 medium, 4 light, and 4 dark triangles.

D: Cut 2 light squares 5⅞″ × 5⅞″. Cut each on the diagonal to make 2 triangles.

E: Cut 1 medium square 5½″ × 5½″.

Slaves brought from Africa were rarely allowed to keep their African names. Renaming slaves was a way of Americanizing them and keeping them symbolically confined in bondage. Richard Jones recalled his aunt, who was born in Africa and kidnapped into slavery: "Judith Gist they named her."[54]

Often slaves were not given more than a first name. When a last name was bestowed, it was usually that of their owner, a practice explained by Mary Divine to a WPA interviewer: "My father's name was James Farrow because he was owned by the Farrows. The slaves had to carry their owners' names, married or not."[55]

When freed, people might adopt a hero's name, such as Washington or Lincoln. A WPA interviewer noted that Rebecca Jane Grant's husband fought in the Union army: "He was known as James Lawton before the war, but became James Lawton Grant after." James Monroe Abbot's name combined the two types of names: a president and the slaveholder. He told a WPA interviewer: "My mother was Allie Ann Lane. After emancipation, I took my daddy's name Abbot—he was Anthony Abbot, and belonged to Joe Abbot, a neighbor."[56]

Children born into slavery often were named by their owners rather than by their mothers. Women might trade the right to name their babies for a piece of cloth, extra rations, or a baby blanket. "My old Missus Hancock named me herself," recalled a former slave in the 1940s, "called me Fillmore Taylor Hancock, after two presidents who took their seats in the 1850s."[57]

Harriet C. Frazier, who studied names in advertisements for Missouri runaways, noted the majority had only a first name. She classified names as biblical, such as Shadrack, Jordan, and Peter, or derived from classical mythology, like Jupiter or Mars. Using surnames for first names, Hampton or Willis, was a naming practice popular with Southern families of all classes. Popular mainstream British first names included George, Harry, and William. Most of the runaways, she noted, were given nicknames. The master might be William or Matthew, but the slave was Bill or Matt.[58]

Certain men's names, like Cuffee and Cujo, are rare echoes of African "day names," from the Akan language in what is now Ghana. Cuffee (*Kofi*) was born on Friday; Cujo (*Kwodwo*), on Monday. Other names like Sambo tended to be such stereotypical names that they became truly negative images. For women, Dorcas, Dinah, and Sukey recur.[59]

Black people, especially in the South, were never addressed as Sir or Ma'am, Mister or Mrs.—titles conferring respect. The accepted form of address for an older black person, free or slave, was aunt or uncle, as in Aunt Jemima or Uncle Tom—names that still smack of servitude.

It is rare to find any quilt pattern names that allude to slavery or seem to be race-related, but a group of about 25 pieced designs appear to echo the old naming traditions. Aunt Dinah's Star, Aunt Jerusha, Aunt Melvernia's Chain, and

Aunt Sukey's pattern may have been the favorite of an aunt truly related by blood, but these names recorded in the early twentieth century do raise interesting questions. The Aunt Dinah block, pictured in a 1946 edition of *Successful Farming* magazine, can symbolize one pervasive aspect of slavery that lingered into the twentieth century.

"Someone's in the kitchen with Dinah
Someone's in the kitchen I know
Someone's in the kitchen with Dinah
Strumming on the old banjo"
—American folk song

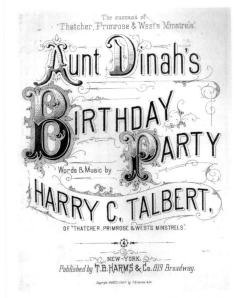

Covers for sheet music from the mid-nineteenth century show how a name such as Dinah became an African-American stereotype. See this unsettling collection on the Library of Congress American Memory website, under the category African-American Sheet Music. Photograph courtesy of the Library of Congress. rpbaasm.0978 (LC-DIG/).

A woman cleans greens on the porch in a classic scene recorded by Rudolph Eickemeyer in the 1890s.[60]

" I have made [baby] Dixie five dresses and have one to make yet.
Then I will have fulfilled my agreement for the privilege of naming her. "

—Slave owner Belle Edmondson, Tennessee, April 29, 1864[61]

This list of slaves, from slaveholder Keziah Brevard's South Carolina diary, shows name types: Biblical, British first names, surnames, nicknames and African day names.

Cora

Cuffe (female)

Dice

Dick

Dorcas

Frank

Hagar

Hampton

Harrison

Harry

Jenny

Jim

Joe

John

Lydia

Mack

Maria

Mary

Ned

Phillis

Rosanna

Sam

Sylvia

Tama

Tom

Violet

Creole Puzzle by Barbara Fife,
Overland Park, Kansas.

Creole Puzzle
A Block to Recall Free Blacks

Mrs. Nancy Lawson, an oil painting by William Matthew Prior
(1806–1873), inscribed May 11, 1843. Mrs. Lawson, in her fashionable
laces, was obviously a free woman of color. Prior also painted a portrait
of Mrs. Lawson's husband. © Shelburne Museum, Shelburne, Vermont.

15″ Block

Level of difficulty: Skilled

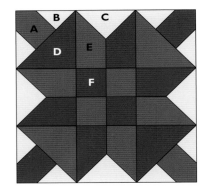

Cutting

A: Cut strips 2⅞″ wide and use template A to cut the 45° angles.

B: Cut 2 light squares 4⅝″ × 4⅝″. Cut on both diagonals to make 4 triangles per square.

C: Cut 1 light square 6¼″ × 6¼″. Cut on both diagonals to make 4 triangles.

D: Cut 1 medium and 1 dark square 5⅞″ × 5⅞″. Cut each on the diagonal to make 2 triangles per square.

E: Cut strips 3″ × 5⅞″. Trim the 45° angles or use the template.

F: Cut 2 dark and 2 medium squares 3″ × 3″.

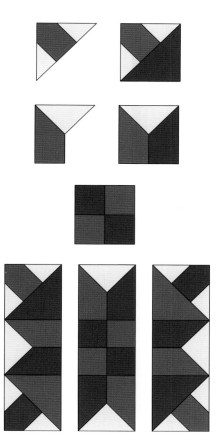

Free people of color have lived in America since early colonial days. By 1810, they amounted to 9 percent of the Southern population. Experiences varied with the era and with the country's cultures, but too many were burdened with racial prejudice. In 1785, an ironic North Carolina law required free blacks to register with town governments and to wear a mandatory shoulder patch emblazoned "Free."

In the years before the Civil War, life became increasingly difficult as some states, even the so-called free states, outlawed free blacks within their borders. By 1850, Missouri, Arkansas, and Delaware were the only Southern states to permit manumission (slaveholders freeing their slaves). These three states allowed the manumitted people to remain. However, ten years later, free people living in Arkansas and Louisiana were ordered to leave or to pick a master.[62]

Black folk in Louisiana, part of the French colonial empire, had once enjoyed a laissez-faire attitude, with more rights and freedom than most African-Americans. Louisiana had long valued its *Creole* legacy, a word meaning a mix of cultures. People with mixed Spanish, French, Native American, or African heritage were all considered Creoles and were proud of their lineage and their style.

A Northern visitor described a stunning black woman seen on a train wearing "an orange and scarlet plaid handkerchief, bound about [her head] Turkish-turban fashion; a style that prevails here among the Creole servants. She had in her ears a pair of gold ear-rings, as large as a half-dollar, plain and massive; she wore a necklace of gold beads, hanging from which was a carnelian cross, the most beautiful thing I ever saw; upon her neck was a richly worked black lace scarf; her dress was plain colored silk, made in the costliest manner … In one hand she held a handsome parasol, and the other fondled a snow-white French poodle upon her lap, said poodle having the tips of its ears tied with knots of pink ribbon and a collar of pink silk."[63]

Life was more austere in Massachusetts for Charlotte Forten, whose parents sent her to school in the heart of abolitionist territory, hoping she'd encounter less prejudice there than in Philadelphia. She wrote sadly in her diary on the first day of school: "There is one young girl and only one—Miss B who I believe thoroughly and heartily appreciates anti-slavery—radical anti-slavery, and has no prejudice against color. I wonder that every colored person is not a misanthrope."[64]

Abolitionist Elizabeth Buffam Chace remembered an insult to a couple on a Boston-bound train: "A well-dressed colored man and his wife [took seats in our railroad car]. The conductor came and ordered the colored people to leave the car. We all remonstrated, of course, but without avail … The colored couple got out quietly, and we did the same, but not so quietly."[65]

Chace's memory was one small moral victory in the long war against segregation and prejudice. Most such stories did not have happy endings. To recall the lives of free blacks, especially those in New Orleans, we can piece Creole Puzzle, designed by Loretta Leitner Rising in 1938 for her "Nancy Cabot" quilt column in the *Chicago Tribune*.

> *[A robin's] music is far sweeter to me than the clearer tones of the Canary birds in their cages, for they are captives, while he is free! I would not keep even a bird in bondage.*

—Charlotte Forten, September 12, 1855

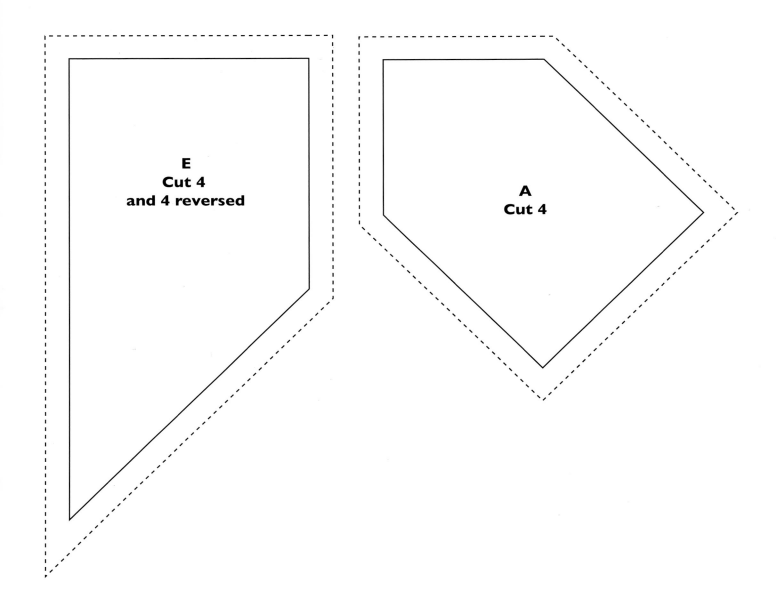

**E
Cut 4
and 4 reversed**

**A
Cut 4**

Jacob's Ladder

A Block to Recall Buying Freedom

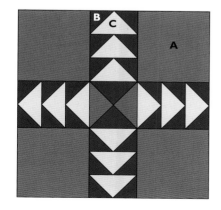

Jacob's Ladder by Pamela Mayfield, Lawrence, Kansas.

In 1864 Atlanta, merchants advertised commodities for sale: china, cigars, and human beings. The man sitting before the auction house has a rifle. He may be a Union soldier guarding the building in the Union-occupied city. Photograph by George N. Barnard, courtesy of the Library of Congress, reproduction number LC-B8171-3608.

15˝ Block

Level of difficulty: Moderate

Cutting

A: Cut 4 medium squares 6⅛˝ × 6⅛˝.

B: Cut 12 dark squares 2¾˝ × 2¾˝. Cut each in half on the diagonal to make 2 triangles per square. You need 24 triangles.

C: Cut 3 light squares 5˝ × 5˝. Cut each on both diagonals cuts to make 4 triangles per square. You need 12 light triangles. Cut 1 medium square 5˝ × 5˝ and 1 dark square 5˝ × 5˝. Cut these into 4 triangles. You only need 2 of each.

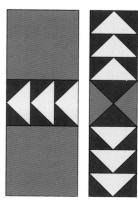

Quilt pattern names are a form of folklore, yet they've been influenced by commercial pattern companies, such as magazine needlework departments and batting and thread manufacturers. Since 1875 or so, copywriters have been choosing catchy names based on a variety of themes. This commercial network is the source for most of our pattern names.

Some names, however, originated with the people who made the quilts. Many traditional names have a religious theme, such as Cross and Crown or Crown of Thorns. Music seems to be the source for others, like Arkansas Traveler. The popular nineteenth-century hobby of botany may be the inspiration for Dusty Miller or Princess Feather, fanciful names for common plants.

Jacob's Ladder is a pattern name that fits all three of these categories: in religion, a graphic Old Testament symbol; in music, a popular American spiritual; and in botany, a native plant. The song is evocative of the whole African-American experience: "We are climbing Jacob's Ladder, Soldiers of the Cross ... Every round goes higher and higher, Soldiers of the Cross."

Jacob's Ladder quilt tops, makers unknown. The pattern can be horizontal or diagonal, with the triangles going away from or toward the center of the block. Other traditional names include Wild Goose Chase and Odd Fellows. The quilt top with the larger blocks is from about 1860. The quilt top with the smaller blocks is from about 1900, when needlework standards had slipped. All the blocks are different sizes, but the quiltmaker solved her problem by adding strips to the smallest blocks.

There are several pieced patterns named Jacob's Ladder. The sampler block, called Jacob's Ladder in a pattern catalog from the Dexter thread company in the 1930s, can symbolize the experience of purchasing one's own freedom, an ascent from slavery made up of many steps. The idea of slaves saving hundreds of dollars by earning their own money, working two or three jobs in addition to the chores of their bondage, is indeed the story of a journey taken one small step at a time.

Elizabeth Hobbs Keckley's tale is often told. Born in Virginia in 1818, she was the daughter of a slave and her white master. Elizabeth learned to sew from her mother. As a teenager, she met a white man who sexually abused her, resulting in the birth of her son, George, born when she was 21. Her owners took her to St. Louis, where Elizabeth's sewing skills earned enough to support the whole family of seventeen people, black and white. This taste of power convinced her she could buy her own freedom. Elizabeth set out to earn and borrow the necessary $1,200.

In 1855, she became a free woman of color, having raised the money to pay for herself and George. The records of the St. Louis Circuit Court show their manumission in November of that year. She sewed to pay back the loans and, five years later, arrived in Washington, D.C., where she opened a dressmaking establishment that eventually employed twenty seamstresses. As a modiste, her most fashionable client was First Lady Mary Lincoln.[66]

A sketch of a slave auction in Richmond, Virginia, from an 1856 London newspaper. Elizabeth Keckley was fortunate that she was permitted to buy herself.

Love of finery was a bond between Elizabeth and Mary, but they had more in common than an interest in elegant clothing. The First Lady and her dressmaker became close friends, sharing grief over the deaths of their sons. Elizabeth lost George in a Missouri battle in 1861. He'd enlisted in the Union army as a white man before black men were permitted to fight. After the Lincolns's boy Willie died of typhoid, Mary had difficulty dealing with her emotional burdens and relied on Elizabeth, the stronger of the pair.

Elizabeth's story is well known because she wrote a best-selling autobiography, but there were many lesser-known tales of people buying themselves, their relatives, or others. Historian Ira Berlin tells of John C. Stanly and Graham Bell, free black men who between them purchased and freed 30 slaves. John B. Metchum bought twenty slaves, who then paid him back for their freedom. Berlin notes—that their "persistence was unusual but not unique."[67]

Portrait of Elizabeth Keckley (1818–1907), from her 1868 book *Behind the Scenes or Thirty Years a Slave and Four Years in the White House.*

"About a week before Christmas I was bridesmaid for Ann Nash; when the night came, I was in quite a trouble; I did not know whether my frock was clean or dirty; I only had a week's notice, and the body and sleeve to make ... I must now close, although I could fill ten pages with my griefs and misfortunes. "

—Letter to her mother by Elizabeth Hobbs, 1838[68]

Climbing Jacob's Ladder

Climbing Jacob's Ladder, pieced and appliquéd by Jean Stanclift. Designed by Barbara Brackman and quilted by Lori Kukuk, Lawrence, Kansas. 2005. 47˝ × 47˝. Jean set five blocks on-point. Over the intersections where the blocks meet, she machine appliquéd a representation of the wildflower named Jacob's ladder.

Jacob's ladder is a member of the phlox family, *Polemonium van-bruntiae,* a pale purple bloom native to the swamps of the East Coast, from Maryland north to New York. Its leaves grow in matched pairs, a ladderlike image that must have reminded botanists of the biblical story of Jacob's vision of angels ascending into heaven. The pieced quilt pattern with its triangles, usually called *Flying Geese,* must have also looked like a celestial ladder to some.

Quilt size: 49½˝ × 49½˝

Block size: 15˝

Border width: 3½˝ finished

You Need

5 Jacob's Ladder blocks

4 half blocks

4 corner triangles

4 border strips

Fabric Requirements

BLOCKS

The quilt is very scrappy, capturing the look of the checks and stripes that were the clothing of slavery but using today's fashionable colors. Our quilt shops carry a wide array of wovens that are perfect for this quilt.

Use scraps from your stash or buy the following:

⅛ yard dark yellow for the floral appliqué

⅛ yard violet for the floral appliqué

¼ yard each of 4 white to tan prints

¼ yard each of 6 light and dark purples—prints plus woven plaids and stripes (Be sure the lights provide some contrast with the whites.)

¼ yard each of 6 light and dark green woven plaids and stripes for edge triangles and the Flying Geese

¼ yard dark green print for the triangles in the Flying Geese

BORDER

1½ yards dark green plaid

BACKING

3 yards

BATTING

Twin size (72˝ × 90˝)

BINDING

½ yard of green stripe

Cutting

CUTTING THE BORDER

Cut 2 strips 4˝ × 43˝ for the top and bottom borders.

Cut 2 strips 4˝ × 50˝ for the side borders.

If you cut the borders first, you can use the leftovers for the blocks.

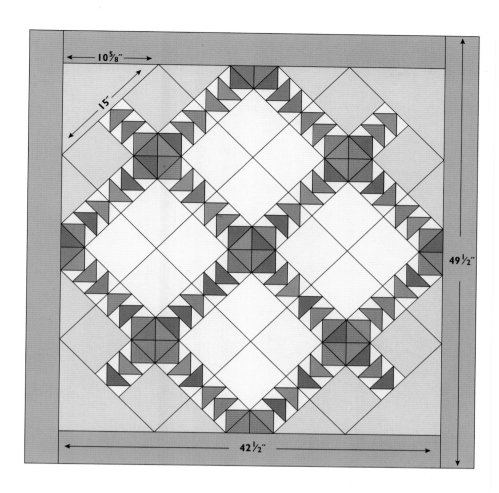

10⅝″

15″

49½″

42½″

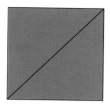

C: Cut 28 squares 5″ × 5″ from a mix of dark purple and dark green fabrics. Cut each on both diagonals to make 4 triangles per square. You need 80 of this larger triangle for the 5 blocks and 32 for the half blocks—112 triangles in all.

D: For the largest triangles in the 4 half blocks around the edge, cut 4 green squares 6½″ × 6½″. Cut each on the diagonal to make 2 triangles per square. You need 8 triangles.

E: For the 4 corner triangles, cut 2 green squares 11½″ × 11½″. Cut each on the diagonal to make 2 triangles per square.

CUTTING THE BLOCKS

Once the quilt top is stitched, it's hard to see the blocks under the appliqué, but there are five Jacob's Ladder blocks set on-point, plus four half blocks along the edges. Use the following color shading to create a central focus and a spot for the appliqué.

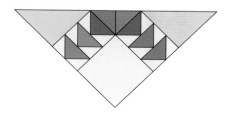

Wash, dry, and press all your fabric. This is very important with woven stripes and plaids, as they tend to shrink more than prints.

Trim off the selvage edges.

A: Cut 16 white and 8 green squares 6⅛″ × 6⅛″. Mix the fabrics for a scrappy look.

B: Cut 84 squares 2¾″ × 2¾″ from a mix of light purple and light green fabrics. Cut each on the diagonal to make 2 triangles per square. You need 120 of the small triangle for the 5 blocks and 48 for the half blocks—168 triangles in all.

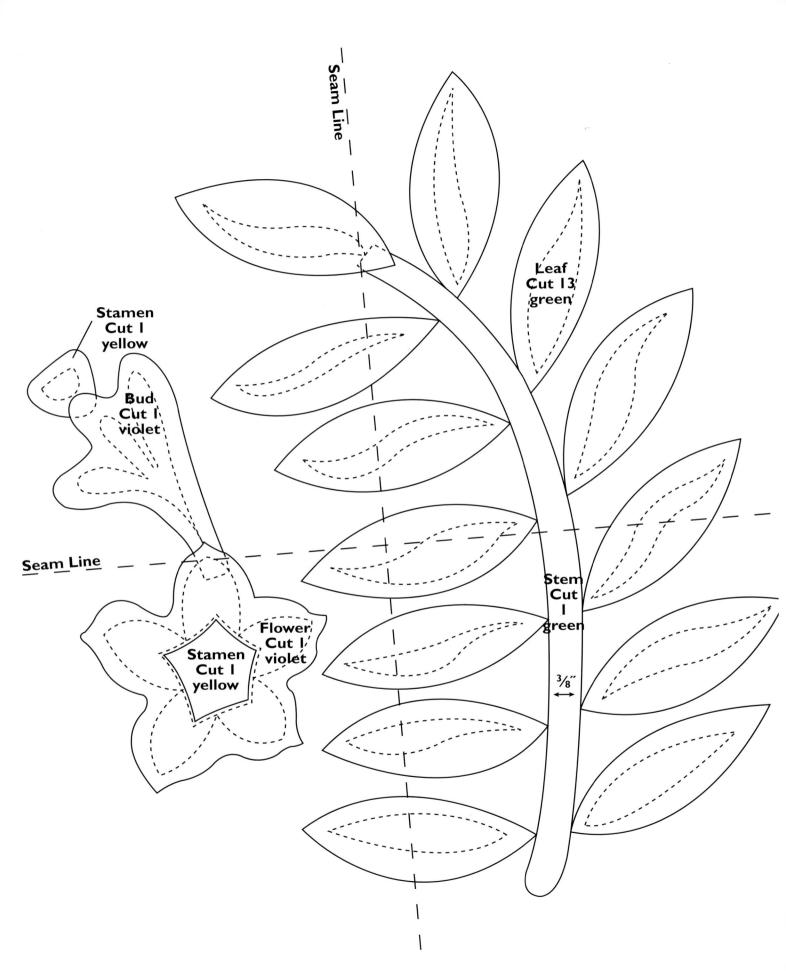

Seam Line

Stamen
Cut 1
yellow

Bud
Cut 1
violet

Leaf
Cut 13
green

Seam Line

Flower
Cut 1
violet

Stamen
Cut 1
yellow

Stem
Cut
1
green

3/8"

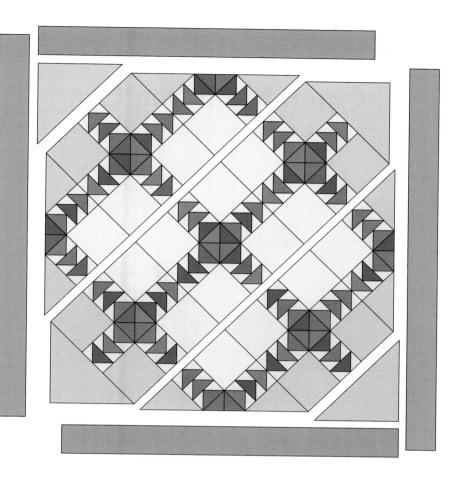

Appliqué

Using the templates, cut leaves and flowers as indicated, adding a scant ¼″ seam allowance as you cut.

Prepare the pieces for appliqué in your favorite manner—basting under or gluing the seam allowances.

Place the pieces over the intersections of the block, as indicated by the dotted lines on the template.

Use your favorite method to appliqué.

Adding the Borders

Add the top and bottom borders and then the sides.

Sewing

PIECING THE BLOCKS

You'll be doing the appliqué *after* the top is set together.

To create the central color focus, you need to piece 1 block with 4 white corners and 4 blocks with variegated corners—white corners on half and green corners on the other.

Piece 4 half blocks.

SETTING THE QUILT

Turn the blocks to create the correct shading with the white squares in the center.

Make 2 strips pieced of 1 block with 2 half blocks.

Make 1 strip of 3 blocks with 2 corner triangles.

Piece these strips together.

Add the last 2 corner triangles.

Newspaper advertisements for runaways often featured a stereotypical woodcut of a man or woman carrying a bundle

Today's storytellers like to imagine a secret code giving potential escapees advice, but these stories are more fabrication than fact. Many people who wrote their own tales of escape recall the event as rather impulsive and, at best, poorly planned. Reverend James W. C. Pennington told his story to a newspaper in 1850. He'd been an enslaved blacksmith in Maryland as a young man, but following a beating,

"Without counsel or assistance, James determined to abscond, and, if possible, reach the free soil of Pennsylvania. One Sunday in November, when all was quiet, he stole away into the woods so ill provided for flight that his little stock of provisions was a morsel of Indian corn bread, about half a pound in weight. Pursuing his way, darkness came on and his only guide was now the North Star, though when or where he should strike Pennsylvania or find a friend, he knew not."

Pennington's journey took days. He found green apples and feed corn to eat, outwitted men determined to capture him by telling them he had been exposed to smallpox, and hid in a barn while a posse of slave hunters offered $200 for his

return to the farmer, who was ignorant of the fugitive hiding a few feet away. Believing he was close to Pennsylvania, he ventured out the next morning onto a public road.

"A little after the sun rose, I came in sight of a toll-gate ... attended only by an elderly woman ... I asked her if I was in Pennsylvania. On being informed that I was, I asked her if she knew where I could get employment. She said she did not, but advised me to go to W___ W___, a Quaker, who lived about three miles from here, whom I would find to take an interest in me."

Pennington stayed with the Quakers for six months and then moved on to New York, where he earned an education in the ministry and became pastor to a black congregation. Like many escapees, he relied on the kindness of strangers, and his intuitive trust of the toll keeper paid off.[74]

Betsy Blakely was also lucky in finding help when she needed it. A slave in Wilmington, North Carolina, "most brutally and basely treated," she fled after hearing a ship was sailing for Boston.

"[She executed] a plan of escape she had long been forming. In the darkness of night, she got, unseen, on board the vessel, and secreted herself in a dark and narrow hole, used for the stowing away of cordage, having provided herself with a bag of bread and a bottle or two of water. There she lay four weeks ... Three or four days before arriving at Boston, she was discovered in her hiding-place by the mate. He learned who she was, and generously supplied her with refreshments. He told no one of her being on board, and on reaching Boston helped her to find a temporary home."[75]

One of the very few stories describing any kind of a secret code was told by Frederick Douglass, recalling his first failed escape plot with friends: "As I now look back, I can see that we did many silly things, very well calculated to awaken suspicion. We were, at times, remarkably buoyant, singing hymns and making joyous exclamations ... A keen observer might have detected in our repeated singing of

O Canaan, sweet Canaan,
I am bound for the land of Canaan,

something more than a hope of reaching heaven. We meant to reach the *North*—and the North was our Canaan."[76]

Sweet Canaan

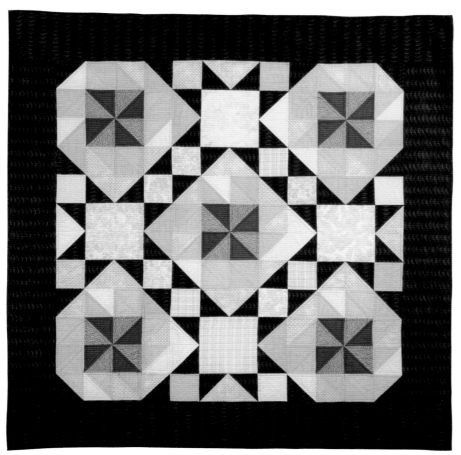

Sweet Canaan, designed by Barbara Brackman, pieced by Jean Stanclift, Lawrence, Kansas, 2005. Machine quilted by Jeanne Zyck. 57″ × 57″.

Frederick Douglass's tale of the double meaning he and his friends assigned to the image of Sweet Canaan—the Promised Land—is the inspiration for this quilt, which combines two blocks, Catch Me If You Can and the North Star. Canaan, on the eastern Mediterranean coast in the Jordan River valley, has long been an important symbol in Jewish lore, in which a literal return from Exodus to the "land of Canaan" was a goal. Christians have also seen Canaan as a once and future spiritual home. To Frederick Douglass in slavery, Canaan meant "the North."

Quilt size: 57″ × 57″

Block size: 15″

Border width: 6″ finished

You Need

5 Catch Me If You Can blocks (pattern on page 68)

4 North Star blocks (pattern on page 84)

4 border strips

Fabric Requirements

BLOCKS

½ yard yellow

½ yard light blue

⅔ yard dark blue (You can use extra fabric from the border.)

1½ yards light green

⅓ yard light purple

⅓ yard dark purple

BORDERS

1¾ yards dark blue

BACKING

2¾ yards cut into strips and pieced, as shown

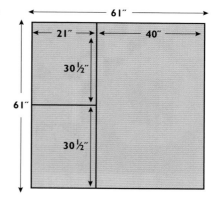

BATTING

Twin size (72″ × 90″)

BINDING

½ yard

Cutting

CUTTING THE BORDERS

Cut 2 dark blue strips 6½″ × 45½″ for the top and bottom borders.

Cut 2 dark blue strips 6½″ × 57½″ for the sides. Use the leftover fabric for the blocks.

Samuel Ringgold Ward wrote of his escape with his parents when he was a boy: "At the time of my parents' escape … [they] did as the few who then escaped mostly did—aim for a free state and settle among Quakers, [who were] regarded as the slave's friend. This peculiarity of their religion they not only held, but so practiced … Obtaining the best directions they could, they set out for Cumberland County, New Jersey, where they had learned slavery did not exist [and] Quakers lived in numbers, who would afford the escaped any and every protection consistent with their peculiar tenets—and where a number of blacks lived, who in cases of emergency could and would make common cause with and for each other."[77]

Harriet Tubman was renowned as an escaped slave who made her way back into the South to help others North. Her New York neighbor, Martha Coffin Wright, wrote a letter describing Tubman's return in 1860:

"We have been expending our sympathies, as well as congratulations, on seven newly arrived slaves that Harriet Tubman has just pioneered safely from the southern part of Maryland … They bought a piece of old comfort and blanket, in a basket with a little kindling, a little bread for the baby with some laudanum, to keep it from crying during the day. They walked all night, carrying the little ones, and spread the old comfort on the frozen ground, in some dense thicket, where they all hid, while Harriet went out foraging and sometimes could not get back till dark, fearing she would be followed … [If] she couldn't find them, we would whistle, or sing certain hymns and they would answer."[78]

Like Douglas, Tubman used hymns as a signal or code. It was well known that she had a price on her head in the South. Other lesser-known conductors on the Underground Railroad also faced punishment from vigilantes and official law enforcement agencies. Some were arrested and served time in prison. More than a few were lynched.

Vintage quilt tops from about 1900. Featured is a small top Barbara made of old blocks. She set them together with a border of a new woven strips. She doesn't often assemble antique blocks because she doesn't like to change their historic nature or stitch into brittle old fabrics, but she couldn't resist the temptation to play with these. The name Underground Railroad for this design was published first by Ruth Finley in her 1929 book *Old Patchwork Quilts and the Women Who Made Them*. Other names include Railroad, Jacob's Ladder, and Road to California. The design was quite popular in about 1900, when magazines and pattern companies bestowed romantic and fanciful names on patterns, both old and new.

Eliza Potter's legal troubles began when she met a frightened young man in Cincinnati, a hotbed of Underground Railroad activity. As a free woman of color, she looked like someone he could trust. Did she know "of a spot on this wide earth where he could be free? I frankly told him all I knew of Canada." He took her advice; his owners pursued him, but "he was beyond their reach and I was pounced upon by them … and arrested as accessory to the deed." Eliza was extradited to Kentucky, where she spent three months in jail. Her eloquent self-defense resulted in an acquittal, and she gladly returned to Ohio.[79]

Minister Hugh Fisher told of his wife's fears that they'd be arrested for aiding a fugitive:

"Charley came to my house. My wife gave him a coverlet and directed him to hide in the weeds until she could send me word to prayer meeting that a refugee was needing our assistance. I arranged for Brother Clayton to pray. I told him to take his time, and he prayed loud and long, while I gave the rescuers word to rally … We concealed the poor fellow, hunted like a wild beast, until the next day, when my wife and Mrs. Weaver dressed him in women's clothes, but unthinkingly gave him a pair of my hose … a beautiful pair with my initials in red in the tops … After his departure it became a source of great alarm to [my wife] lest he should be captured and through the initialed socks she and Mrs. Weaver be discovered."[80]

Follow the Drinking Gourd

Follow the Drinking Gourd pieced by Barbara Brackman and friends, Lawrence, Kansas, 2004. Machine quilted by Rosie Mayhew. 78˝ × 93˝.

Follow the Drinking Gourd is an old spiritual—Harriet Tubman's favorite. The song can be interpreted in many ways. The Drinking Gourd was a name for the constellation also called the Big Dipper, which points to the age-old navigational tool, the North Star. The lyrics might refer to a spiritual home in a heaven beyond the stars, or they might give directions to earthly freedom in the North.

The pattern is an original. The Women Who Run With Scissors, a small sewing group, decided to trade blocks for quilts that chained in some fashion; Barbara designed this block, based on two traditional patterns—the North Star and the Underground Railroad—and collected 20 blocks from group members.

Barbara's poetic license allowed her to choose symbolic colors. The theme is Butternut and Blue, an echo of the Civil War, with the golden brown representing the homespun fabric of the Confederacy and the blue representing the Union. The colors also represent the gold of the starry constellations in the dark night sky. The lighter ivory squares in the four-patches can be seen as a trail or road illuminated by the underlying North Star. Barbara asked her friends to choose prints from their stashes, ensuring a very scrappy look.

Trip Around the World by Barbara Fife, Overland Park, Kansas.

Trip Around the World

A Block to Recall Colonization

A daguerreotype of a Liberian woman, possibly Mrs. Urias Africanus McGill. The woman holds a daguerreotype in her lap, perhaps a photograph of a deceased relative. This photograph was taken by Augustus Washington (1820–1875), a free African-American who opened his first studio in Hartford, Connecticut. In 1853, he took his family to Liberia, where he met the McGills, who'd emigrated twenty years earlier. Urias McGill had lived in Monrovia since he was eight and prospered as a merchant there. Washington also achieved success in Liberia as a sugarcane planter and politician. Photograph courtesy of the Library of Congress (call # US26-1949).

15″ Block

Level of difficulty: Moderate

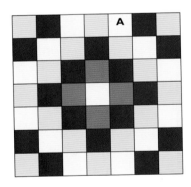

Cutting

A: Cut 13 light, 16 medium light, 4 medium dark, and 16 very dark squares $2\frac{5}{8}'' \times 2\frac{5}{8}''$.

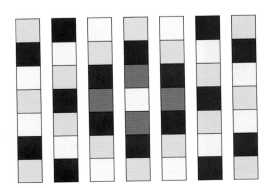

One step in the process toward emancipation was a national movement called Colonization, which developed early in the nineteenth century. Many people believed freed and escaped slaves should move to colonies established in Canada, which had eliminated slavery with a program of gradual emancipation. The obvious advantage to colonies in Canada was the country's proximity. A slave running north into Ohio or Pennsylvania need only make it across the Great Lakes.

The disadvantages to Canadian colonies were the climate and the sparseness of the population, characteristics that were often exaggerated in the South to scare slaves who dreamed of asylum. In 1859, escapee Jackson Whitney had the satisfaction of writing his former owner: "I am comfortably situated in Canada … The country is not what it has been represented to me and others to be. In place of its being cold and barren, it has beautiful, comfortable climate." Whitney requested that the slave owner release his family. "You must not consider that is a slave talking to 'massa' now, but one as free as yourself."[81]

Another idea, popular for a while, was a "back to Africa" movement. In 1817, George Washington Parke Custis, grandson of Martha Washington, helped organize the American Colonization Society, which purchased land in Africa that eventually became the country of Liberia. At that time, ten years after the African slave trade was outlawed in the United States, many American slaves had been born in Africa and may have nurtured hopes they might return. As the decades wore

on, however, and African-born generations died out, few black people native to the United States had any desire to relocate to Africa. Many believed Colonization to be a wrongheaded and bigoted concept.

Rosabella Burke and her family left America for Liberia in 1854. She wrote letters to her former owner, Mary Custis Lee, George Washington Parke Custis's daughter and the wife of then U.S. Army officer Robert E. Lee. Rosabella's first letter after a few months was positive about the climate and the culture, which was more American than African. After five years, she remained enthusiastic: "Remember me kindly to Aunt Elleanor, tell her that I love Africa and would not exchange it for America."[82]

The Trip Around the World block, an arrangement of squares into a mosaic-like pattern, was popular in Pennsylvania about 1900, where it was a folk pattern passed from quilter to quilter. The Pennsylvania Germans also called it Rainbow. The design can recall the journey of families like the Burkes, who sought to escape not only slavery but also American bigotry.

Trip to the Kalahari, machine pieced and quilted by Lavon E. Wynn, Kansas City, Kansas, 2005. 40˝ × 40˝.

Lavon's version of the Trip Around the World pattern takes it far from its Pennsylvania folk origins. She incorporated animal prints of all kinds—zebra stripes and tortoise shell, leopard spots and snakeskin— and pieced four identical blocks with 2˝ sashing and two borders—a narrow 1˝ inner border and a 3˝ outer border. After seeing a nature program on zebras in their natural habitat, Lavon and Barbara named this quilt for Africa's Kalahari Desert. The set is similar to My African Trip (page 19).

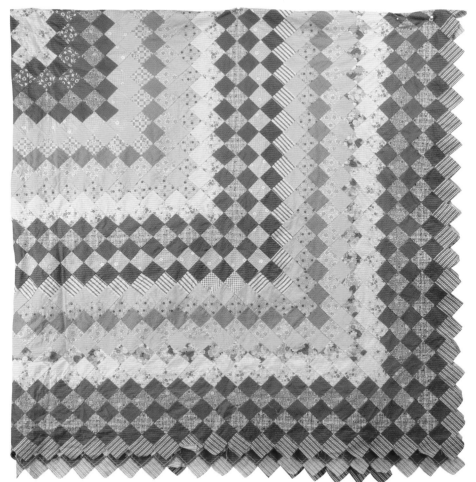

Trip Around the World by Mrs. Olsen, Salinas, California, 1948, one-quarter view of unquilted top.

What began as a folk pattern was adopted by the commercial quilt pattern network in the mid-twentieth century, when many magazines and retailers offered patterns and kits for variations of the design. A label on this quilt top states that it was made in Salinas in 1948 by "a Mrs. Olsen, who was visiting from Kansas. The fabric is 1930's J.C. Penney 'Rondo' prints (29 cents per yard)."

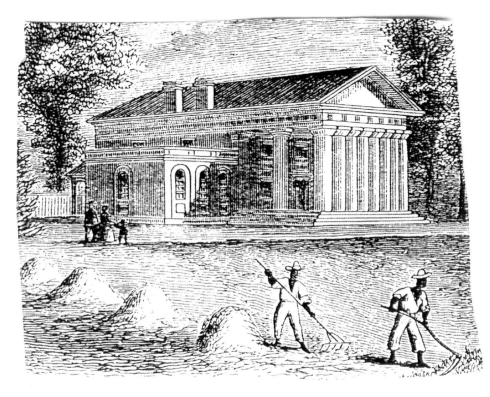

Rosabella Burke was a slave on the Custis-Lee plantation in Virginia, where the main house was a showpiece of Greek revival architecture. To punish the family of General Robert E. Lee during the Civil War, the federal government confiscated the plantation for the Union grave-yard we now call Arlington National Cemetery.

Box Quilt

A Block to Recall the Abolitionist Movement

A portrait of Sojourner Truth during the Civil War. Isabella Baumfree (1797–1883) was born a slave in New York and spoke Dutch as her first language. After she was freed by the state's gradual emancipation law, she was inspired to devote her life to the antislavery cause, adopting a new name to symbolize her mission. Her 1850 autobiography, *The Narrative of Sojourner Truth: A Northern Slave,* and her dramatic speaking style made her a star on the abolitionist lecture circuit. Photograph courtesy of the National Portrait Gallery, Smithsonian Institution (NPG.78.207).

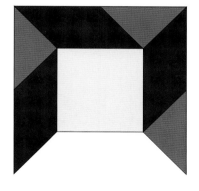

Box Quilt by Pamela Mayfield, inked by Barbara Brackman, Lawrence, Kansas.

15˝ Block

Level of difficulty: Moderate

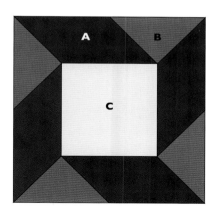

Cutting

A: Cut 4 dark rectangles 4¼˝ × 12½˝. Use the template to cut the 45° angles.

B: Cut 1 medium square 8¾˝ × 8¾˝. Cut on both diagonals to make 4 triangles.

C: Cut 1 light square 8˝ × 8˝. This is the perfect place to sign and date your quilt, so pick something that will highlight your signature.

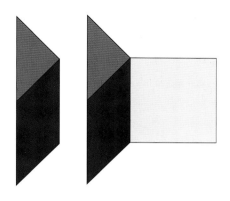

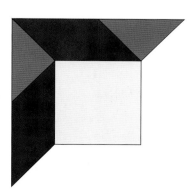

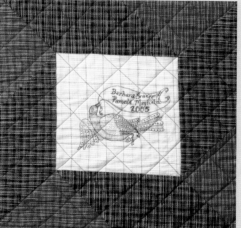

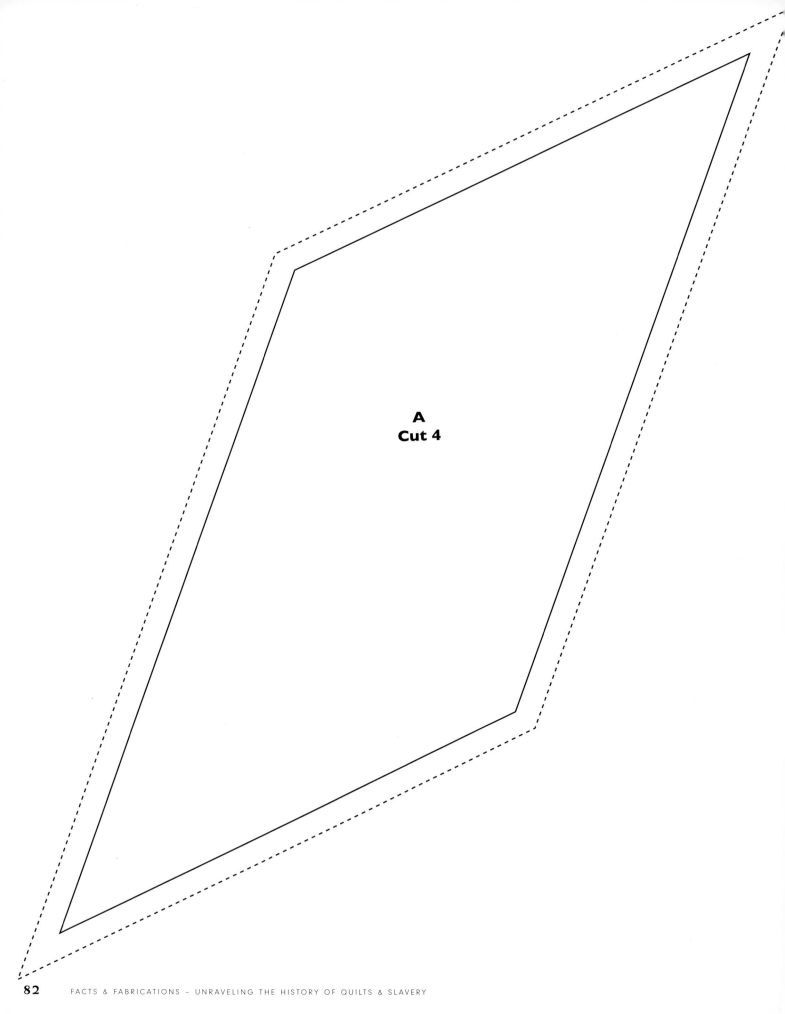

A
Cut 4

Ideas about gradual emancipation and Colonization gave way to more militant cries for immediatism, the abolition of slavery with no waiting period and no monetary compensation for slaveholders. People who believed slavery to be a moral, religious, or economic wrong that must be eliminated at any cost came to be called abolitionists.

While Frederick Douglass was a slave in Maryland, he first heard the word abolitionist from the whites on the plantation. They were, Douglass remarked, "speaking with much warmth and excitement about 'abolitionists.' Of who or what these were I was totally ignorant. I found, however, that whatever they might be, they were most cordially hated and soundly abused by slaveholders." He found the "incendiary information" he was looking for in a Baltimore newspaper, where he read of abolitionists petitioning Congress, "praying for the abolition of slavery in the District of Columbia and for the abolition of the slave trade between the states of the Union. This was enough … There was HOPE in those words."[83]

Henry "Box" Brown uncrated in Philadelphia

Antislavery activists were usually painted with the same broad brush, especially by Southerners incensed by their ideas. However, the movement sheltered many sects— some who believed the Northern states should immediately secede from the Union; others who advocated only the stabilization of slavery in the Deep South, with no expansion into the new states forming in the West. Some activists believed in electing like-minded politicians. More radical abolitionists refused to vote at all.

Abolitionists of all stripes believed in the power of the word to transform society's attitude. The word was written, as in the petitions with which they besieged Congress, and published in pamphlets, books, and newspapers that rolled out of Northern printing presses. The word was also spoken. Abolitionists sponsored a highly effective speaker's bureau that sent lecturers throughout the North.

Many well-meaning Northerners deluded themselves into believing that slaves were happy in their station, that a slave was not self-reflective enough to be aware of his or her condition. Abolitionists hoped to arouse empathy for people in slavery by introducing ignorant audiences to educated and eloquent African-Americans. Escaped slaves who spoke of their experiences drew crowds to the lecture halls.

A logo of the abolitionist movement, which appeared on everything from quilts to china

Henry Brown's escape strategy was marvelously simple. He built a wooden crate and shipped himself from Virginia to Philadelphia. "Box" Brown's lectures were entertaining as well as inspiring. He often brought the crate on stage. He was one of about a hundred refugees who published books about their personal experiences in slavery between 1760 and 1865. People who claimed ignorance about the slave's humanity had no excuse not to learn.[84]

The Box Quilt was pictured in the 1890 catalog from the Ladies' Art Company, a St. Louis firm that sold mail-order patterns. The design can represent abolitionists, like Sojourner Truth and Henry Brown, who worked to change attitudes one mind at a time.

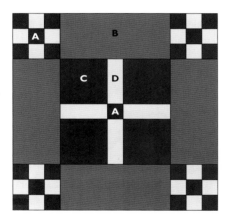

Beauregard Surrounded by Pamela Mayfield, Lawrence, Kansas.

Beauregard Surrounded
A Block to Recall the Civil War

Two men in Union uniforms sit before a shell-proof dugout, about 1865. Photograph courtesy of the Library of Congress, reproduction number LC-USZ62-118353.

15″ Block

Level of difficulty: Beginner

Cutting

A: Cut 21 dark and 16 light squares 1⅝″ × 1⅝″.

B: Cut 4 medium rectangles 8¾″ × 3⅞″.

C: Cut 4 dark squares 4″ × 4″.

D: Cut 4 light rectangles 1⅝″ × 4″.

(***Note:*** See the Tip on page 90 with the *Beauregard Surrounded* quilt project for more instructions about making this block.)

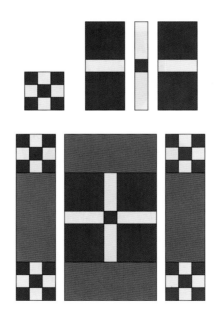

The Civil War officially began in April 1861 in South Carolina when Confederate troops assaulted Fort Sumter in Charleston's harbor.

The war lasted four years, a terrible event in American history but a glorious deliverance to the slaves. This sampler recalls the war by including a simple block that looks much like a woven coverlet. In 1890, the *Ohio Farmer* recorded the name Beauregard's Surroundings, probably for Confederate General Pierre Beauregard. It's better known by the name Burgoyne Surrounded, a reference to a British general in the American Revolution. This adaptation combines both names to symbolize a May, 1862 Civil War battle in Corinth, Mississippi, that left Beauregard's forces in retreat and the Union army in control of a corner of Mississippi.

Confederate General Pierre Gustave Toutant Beauregard

Beauregard was *the* Southern hero in the Civil War's first year—the victor at Fort Sumter and at the Confederate rout in Manassas. A star-struck Virginian, Fannie Page Hume, helped a friend send a handmade shirt to the general:

"June 20, 1861. We sent Gen'l Beauregard the flannel shirt by Mrs. Taylor today. I wrote the note.

June 21, 1861. Oh wonder of wonders!!! A bona fide note from Gen'l Beauregard thanking us for the shirt and the complimentary mention of the 'Daughters of the South.' I was never more excited."[89]

Beauregard's star descended with losses at Shiloh and Corinth. He was replaced in Southern hearts by Thomas "Stonewall" Jackson and Robert E. Lee. After Beauregard's loss at Corinth, Union troops settled into Mississippi, and the town of Corinth became a magnet for runaway slaves seeking protection. Earlier in the war, when a Virginian had the gall to request the return of his slaves from

Union General Benjamin Butler under U.S. law, Butler pointed out that secessionists had no federal rights. Slaves were war's "contraband" and could be confiscated and freed. Thus, the name *Contraband* became widely used to mean a former slave.

Crowds of Contraband refugees followed Union armies throughout the South. Georgeanna Woolsey, a Union nurse, wrote her mother from a boat in Virginia, describing "the spontaneous movement of the slaves, who … came flocking from all the country about, bringing their little moveables, frying pans, old hats, and bundles to the river side. There was no appearance of anxiety or excitement among them. Fortunately there was plenty of deck room for them on the forage boats, one of which, as we passed, seemed filled with women only, in their gayest dresses and brightest turbans, like a whole load of tulips for a horticultural show … Now and then the roar of the battle came to us, but the slave women were quietly nursing their children and singing hymns. The day of their deliverance had come and they accepted the most wonderful change with absolute placidity."[90]

"[Mr. Harrison's slaves] have left him except the cook and two of her children. Maria says colored people were at first as hot secesh as the 'white folks.'—'I outdid Mrs. Harrison,' [she said], but since the Union army has been there, 'We know better.'"

—Elizabeth Blair Lee in Maryland, 1862[91]

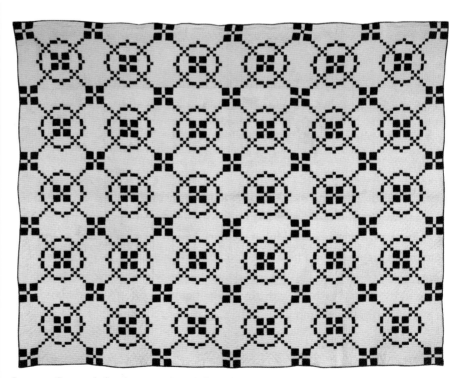

Burgoyne Surrounded, unknown maker, 1840–1880. This quilt was pictured in Ruth Finley's 1929 book *Old Patchwork Quilts and the Women Who Made Them*, in which she called it Road to California or Wheel of Fortune. Collection of the Dague family.

Tip

If you stitch these with perfect accuracy, you'll have $3\frac{7}{8}'' \times 3\frac{7}{8}''$ squares with the seams allowed. Because you'll be setting these to 4" strips, you will need to do a tiny adjustment when you sew the seams. The nine-patches will have a $\frac{3}{16}''$ seam allowance, rather than the usual $\frac{1}{4}''$. Once you get into the habit of setting the $3\frac{7}{8}''$ nine-patch next to the 4" pieces with that fudge factor, you'll have no problem getting everything to square up.

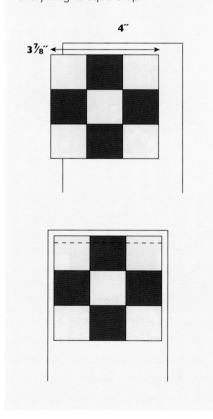

SEWING THE BLOCKS

Stitch the blocks as shown in the diagram, using 4 nine-patches in each block.

You need 16 blocks.

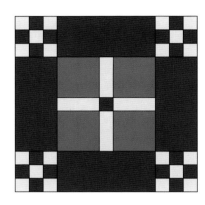

Setting the Blocks

Make 4 strips of 4 blocks and 4 sashing strips.

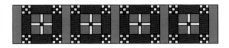

Make 5 units of 4 sashing strips and 5 small nine-patches.

Stitch the rows together.

The Borders

Take all the leftover 4" blue strips you have and sew those random lengths into border strips.

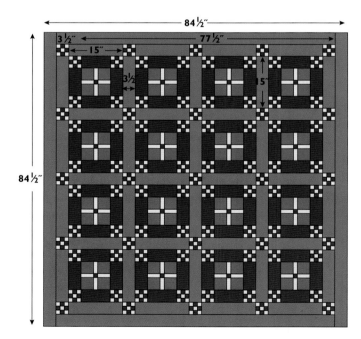

You need 2 strips $4'' \times 78''$ for the top and bottom borders and 2 strips $4'' \times 85''$ for the sides.

Add the top and bottom borders and then the sides.

Lincoln's Platform

A Block to Recall the Emancipation Proclamation

Lincoln's Platform (variation) by Susan Burghart, Bentonville, Arkansas.

Eliza Brown with George Armstrong Custer and Elizabeth Bacon Custer in a studio portrait taken April 12, 1865, three days after the Confederate army's formal surrender at Appomattox and two days before Abraham Lincoln's assassination. Photograph courtesy of the Little Bighorn Battlefield National Monument.

15″ Block

Level of difficulty: Beginner

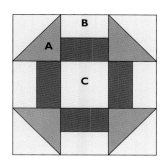

Cutting

A: Cut 2 dark and 2 light squares 5⅞″ × 5⅞″. Cut each on the diagonal to make 2 triangles per square. You need 4 dark and 4 light triangles.

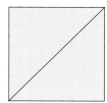

B: Cut 4 medium and 4 light rectangles 5½″ × 3″.

C: Cut 1 light square 5½″ × 5½″.

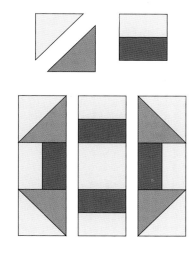

For most white Northerners, the Civil War's major objective was the Union's preservation. President Abraham Lincoln, whose election prompted South Carolina to secede, was opposed to slavery but initially determined that emancipation was not federal policy. When General John C. Frémont issued a proclamation freeing the slaves in Missouri early in the war, Lincoln rescinded the order and demoted Frémont.

After more than a year of war, Lincoln changed his mind and issued the Emancipation Proclamation, which stated that from January 1, 1863, all slaves in rebel states were free. The measure was more symbolic than effective, as the federal government had little influence in Confederate states. Slavery in Missouri, Maryland, and Kentucky, border states that had not seceded, was unchanged. The symbolism, however, was important, announcing that slavery's abolition was a Union goal.

President Abraham Lincoln

Lincoln's proclamation made little immediate difference to most slaves, who didn't hear of it until the end of the war. But George Bolinger, interviewed during the WPA project, remembered, "When Mister Lincoln made his proclamation (that was before the war was over) young master Dave set us free. He gave us a yoke of oxen and a wagon full of everything we needed. There was a feather bed and quilts and meat and provisions."[92]

Bolinger's memory seems a bit nostalgic in contrast to that of fourteen-year-old Sarah, a Florida refugee who told her story to teacher Esther Hill Hawk: "Sarah shows more bitterness in speaking of her old mistress than I have ever seen in any of them. She says, 'I'll always hate her because she never gave me enough to eat, not till it spoiled when she done had enough.' The greatest incentive which she has to learn [to read and write] is that she may be able to write to her old mistress to tell her that she 'has bacon and hominy and rice too, all I can eat, and if you come here I'd like to see you starve.' "[93]

Seventeen-year-old Eliza Brown walked away from slavery in Rappahannock County, Virginia, in August 1863. Her memories of the day were captured in Elizabeth Bacon Custer's book *Tenting on the Plains*: "After the Emancipation, everybody was standing up for liberty, and I wasn't going to stay home when everybody else was goin'." She also told Custer that people on the plantation were hungry. The armies had confiscated everything edible: "So I lit out, 'cause there'd be one less mouth to feed."

Eliza Brown cooking under fire

possibly established in the folklore; others might have been the whim of a copywriter. Carrie Hall, in her 1935 book, named this block Lincoln's Platform, recalling the president who held the Union together with the force of his convictions and who eventually freed the slaves. His murder, just days after Lee's surrender, placed Lincoln firmly in American myth. Seventy-five years later, when Annie Bridges, who'd been born into slavery, was interviewed during the WPA project, she remembered a rhyme:

"If it hadn't been for Uncle Abraham
What would we have done?
Been down in the cotton field
Picking in the sun."[95]

"
Everybody was excited over freedom, and I wanted to see how it was. Everybody keeps asking me why I left. I can't see why they can't recollect what the war was for, and that we were all bound to try and see for ourselves how it was. "

—Eliza Brown Davison, interview with Elizabeth Custer, 1886

Eliza left her three-year-old son, John, at home and joined several others from her plantation in a Union army camp. "We were standing around waiting," when she met Brigadier General George Armstrong Custer, looking among the Contrabands for a cook. The 23-year-old soldier and the 17-year-old escapee agreed she would join his entourage. She spent the rest of the war traveling with the Union army, "a marvel of courage," according to the general's wife. Eliza stayed with the Custers after the Civil War, accompanying them to Texas and Kansas until 1869, when she moved to Ohio, retrieved son John, and married lawyer Andrew Jackson Davison. Eliza and Elizabeth worked together on Elizabeth's best-selling memoirs of life with General Custer, in which she wrote, "Eliza's story of her war life is too long for these pages." Fortunately, Elizabeth did record some of Eliza's memories of emancipation: "I always thought … that I didn't sit down to wait to have them all free *me*. I helped to free myself."[94]

The block called Lincoln's Platform is one seen often in quilts made during Eliza's time. When magazines and pattern companies began selling patterns, they gave this block many names—Double Monkey Wrench, Churn Dash, Hens and Chickens, Sherman's March, and Shoo Fly. Some of these names were

Birds in the Air (variation) by Charlotte Enfield, Bentonville, Arkansas.

Birds in the Air
A Block to Recall Freedom

Katherine Foote Coe of Connecticut and two unnamed students in South Carolina. After food, shelter, and clothing, education was a priority. Many Northern women traveled to the South during and after the war to teach freed people to read and write in schools protected by Union troops. The freed women are dressed in what were probably hand-me-downs—bold patterns that had been popular a decade earlier. Photograph courtesy of the Stowe-Day Foundation.

15˝ Block

Level of difficulty: Moderate

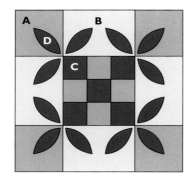

Cutting

A: Cut 4 medium squares 4¼˝ × 4¼˝.

B: Cut 4 light rectangles 4¼˝ × 8˝.

C: Cut 4 medium and 5 dark squares 3˝ × 3˝.

D: Use the template to cut 12 dark pieces, adding a scant ¼˝ seam allowance to the shape as you cut.

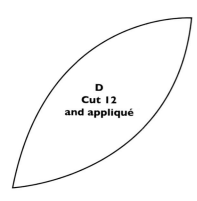

D
Cut 12
and appliqué

Appliqué

Piece the block first, as shown in the diagram.

Prepare piece D by turning under the edges and basting or gluing as you like.

Position the ovals diagonally on piece A, with the corner squares as shown. Baste or glue them in place.

Repeat for the rectangles (piece B).

Use your favorite appliqué method to stitch the ovals.

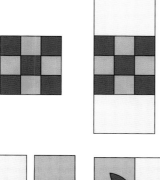

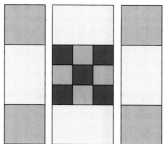

Blue Birds by Barbara Brackman, Lawrence, Kansas, 2005. Machine quilted by Rosie Mayhew. 47″ × 47″.

The reproduction quilt on the wall is pictured with an antique top that looks to date from about 1850. The four-patch design set with triangles is a strip version of the Underground Railroad block (page 73). The school supplies recall a letter written by Rebecca Primus in 1862, describing a charity ball staged by New York City's African-American community. Profits would "go towards purchasing books and slates [for the Contraband]."[96]

Barbara used reproduction fabrics to give a nineteenth-century look to this four-block quilt, a color palette similar to the dresses worn by the students in the photograph on page 94. The "birds"—the appliquéd leaflike shapes—are bluebirds cut from a rainbow print with swirls of dark and bright blue. For instructions on setting a quilt with four blocks and a 3″ sashing, see page 19. To take advantage of the repeat in the chintz, Barbara enlarged the border to finish to 7″ and mitered the corners.

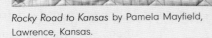

Rocky Road to Kansas

A Block to Recall the Exodusters

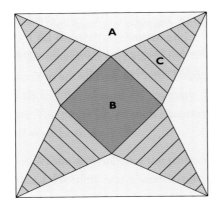

Rocky Road to Kansas by Pamela Mayfield, Lawrence, Kansas.

15˝ Block

Level of difficulty: Moderate

Cutting

A and C: Use the templates (page 102) to cut pieces A and C.

Note that piece A is double the size of the pattern piece.

Note that piece C is cut from striped fabric.

B: Cut 1 medium square 5¾˝ × 5¾˝.

The Shores family of Custer County, posing in 1887 before their sod house for photographer Solomon Butcher, who documented Nebraska's pioneers. Jerry Shores, sitting to the left of the family's terrier, was a former slave who led a black emigrant train west. Other family members include Minerva Shores on the left, with her baby; the Reverend Marks; Jerry's wife, Rachel; and (standing) their son, Jim. Free land on the Great Plains inspired many to take a chance on new lives. Photograph courtesy of the Nebraska Historical Society.

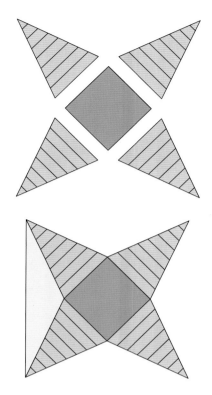

Once joy over freedom and victory was exhausted, emancipation disappointed many. Years wasted arguing about gradualism versus immediatism and compensation versus abolition, plus the stubbornness of Southern slaveholders, resulted in no real plan for readjustment for freed people. Many former slaves walked away from their homes with nothing into a shattered Southern economy. The federal government sent troops into the South to protect the African-Americans, to ensure their rights, and to "reconstruct" the local governments. After more than a decade of little improvement, however, federal troops left in 1877, and most ex-slaves faced bleak futures.

Eliza Madison remembered Reconstruction in a WPA interview: "After the war was over we all worked for 25 cents a day but didn't get paid in money, but in food." Poverty was not the only hardship. Other interviewees recalled the terrorism of vigilante gangs. Frederick Ross told interviewers of attempts to intimidate the people in his Missouri neighborhood: "One time the Ku Klux came around. They knocked on the door and they said 'Please give me a drink. I ain't had a drink since the Battle of Shiloh.' Why did they say that? Why you see, they wanted us to think they were the spirits of the soldiers killed at Shiloh and they'd been in hell so long they drank all the water they can get."[104]

Nate Fitz told interviewers in a 2004 newspaper article that his great-grandfather, Alford Teal, left Texas, where "the sharecropping system ... was so similar to slavery." The Teals decided to move to Kansas, a place that had achieved mythical status as a free territory in the years before the Civil War. In the late 1870s, Kansas offered free homesteads, as well as the symbolic memory of liberty. The Teals were not alone. Kansas Fever inflamed the South. In a spontaneous migration in 1879 and 1880, an estimated 20,000 African-Americans left the South for Kansas, Nebraska, and other newly opened plains states.[105]

A woman photographed waiting for her day's pick of cotton to be weighed, about 1900. She was paid 50 cents for each 100 pounds. For many, life in the South changed very little after the Civil War. This photograph was published in a 1906 book titled *Cotton, Its Cultivation, Marketing, Manufacture, and the Problems of the Cotton World.*

Rocky Road to Kansas by an unknown maker, 1890–1920.
The design, a favorite at the turn of the twentieth century,
is also known as Lazy Gal and Kite. A Saint Louis pattern
business, the Ladies' Art Company, sold the pattern through
the mail as Rocky Road to Kansas beginning in about 1890,
a decade after the great exodus. The star points are
traditionally pieced of small scraps called "strings," but
striped fabric gives the same effect with less work. Notice
the single block with the red strips and how orderly it seems
compared with the others. The maker may have been given
a block to copy and then did her own version in the other
41 blocks.

This cased photograph, from the collection of the Kansas State Historical Society, features an unknown woman. Her dress and the photography technique indicate the picture was taken in about 1860. She may have sat for the photograph in Kansas, a refuge for escapees running from the neighboring slave state of Missouri, or the memento may have been carried with a family moving west after the war.

Because their travels echoed the story of the Jews' flight from Egypt in the Book of Exodus, the emigrants became known as *Exodusters*. Falsely believing they were entitled to a mule, 40 acres, and farming equipment, many were unprepared for the hardships of getting a new start in a marginal climate. Large refugee camps grew up in St. Louis and Kansas City along the rivers and railroads. Yet few turned back. Many determined pioneers decided that whatever awaited them on their own small dry-land farms was far better than post–Civil War life in the South. The Exodusters founded numerous colonies throughout the Great Plains.

Kansas was home to Morton City, Hill City, Dunlap, and Nicodemus, among others. The Teal family and 25 other Texas families wound up in Votaw. Twine and Langston in Oklahoma and Brownlee and De Witty in Nebraska were other Exoduster towns. Many of these towns eventually succumbed to flood, drought, or the depression.

The Rocky Road to Kansas pattern can remind us of the Great Exodus of 1879. Like the wagon trains of the 1850s and the dust bowl refugees of the 1930s, it was a mass migration that changed America.

Rocky Road Medallion by Gloria A. Clark, Kansas City, Kansas, 2005. 68˝ × 68˝. Gloria's collection of ethnic fabrics, including scraps from her wardrobe, is the foundation for this quilt based on four Rocky Road blocks. She learned to make quilts as a young woman, after the grandmother she calls "Big Mommy" told the girl cousins that when they planned to marry, she would sew each a quilt if the girl would help her. Gloria was the only cousin to take advantage of the sewing lessons. That quilt is long gone, worn out in raising a family. Today Gloria is making quilts again, inspired by the memory of her grandmother.

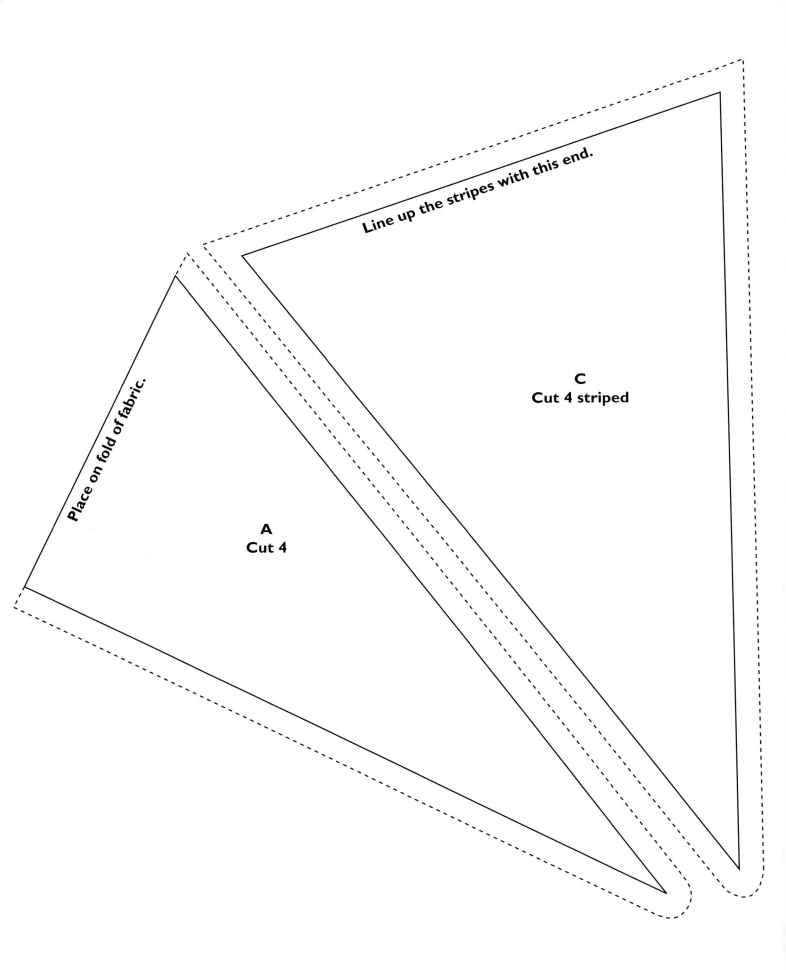

Line up the stripes with this end.

C
Cut 4 striped

Place on fold of fabric.

A
Cut 4

CHAPTER 5

Adapting the Sampler for Children

Jacob's Ladder, pieced and hand quilted by Linda Birch Mooney, Shawnee, Kansas, 2005. 40″ × 40″.

Linda redrafted thirteen of the sampler blocks to 6″ squares and set them on-point with a 2″ blue sashing and a 3″ blue border. The colors are dark, a subdued version of red, white, and blue, to remember a dark period in our national history.

Quiltmaking is in excellent way to interest children in history while also teaching sewing skills. Making a quilt, whether it's a small square to cover a teddy bear or a full-sized group project, gives children a powerful sense of accomplishment. If the quilt is associated with an equally powerful tale of American history, the lessons learned will not be forgotten.

Although this book is for adults, the sewing lessons and the history lessons are easily adapted for children as young as the early elementary grades. Each sampler block has a skill level indicated. Blocks 2, 3, 8, 9, 13, 16, 17, and 18 are all beginner blocks. This skill level is based on the type of seams and the number of pieces. These eight blocks are probably the best to use with children.

You might want to preview the stories before you read them aloud to very young children. Violence and abuse are, unfortunately, an important part of the story of slavery, but the stories linked to the quilt blocks do not dwell on either. Many stories end on an uplifting note that helps explain how people overcame adversity.

Needlework teachers might want to use the stories and blocks in this book to teach classes for children at quilt shops or history museums. I used several of the simpler blocks to teach a sewing club that met weekly after school. In the club, kids made a small quilt of four sampler blocks, set as shown on page 19. During the classes, we talked about local history and the story of slavery, reading tales of the Underground Railroad aloud as we sewed. The children gained sewing skills (we used machines and rotary cutters with older kids) and a new understanding of the personal testimony behind history.

The sampler blocks and the stories included with them can also be adapted for elementary school teachers. I've helped teachers organize a curriculum around the story of slavery for a larger group. We asked volunteers and parents to come in once a week and work with groups of two and three hand stitchers. Kids made blocks for a full-sized quilt and the volunteers finished the top, which the class then tied on a frame.

Members of the Mooney-Pettway family pose together at a treadle sewing machine in this 1937 photograph by Arthur Rothstein. The Farm Security Administration took many photographs in Gee's Bend, Alabama, home to one of American quiltmaking's great regional traditions. Photograph courtesy of the Library of Congress, reproduction number LC-USF34-025363D.

Parents and home schoolers can use this book as a one-on-one cooperative project. A team of a grown-up and a child can make blocks, read the stories, and discuss the history of slavery. This team method—patchwork partners—works very well with beginning stitchers making a small doll quilt, as described on page 106.

Discussion Questions

Many good curricula on the topic of slavery are available for children. These curricula include discussion questions that can lead to a better understanding of the topic. The following questions are designed to be used with this book, particularly in relation to the photographs and the quilt blocks.

Question 1: We can learn a lot by looking carefully at photographs to study how the people are posed, what they are wearing, and the expressions on their faces. When we look at the people in the old photographs, most of them seem to be very serious. Why do you think they look so serious?

Possible answers: They may be sad; life in slavery was difficult and joys were few. They may be nervous; people were not used to having their pictures taken. It's also good to remember that they had to hold still for quite a long time so they wouldn't look blurred in the picture. Having one's picture taken was a serious event. Very few people smiled in their pictures in the mid-nineteenth century. They wanted to be remembered as solemn.

A sketch titled "The Brothers Assisted in the Quilting" from an 1883 edition of *Harper's Magazine* pokes gentle fun at men trying to thread their needles. The cartoon shows people's humorous side, something that rarely appeared in photographs until the twentieth century.

Question 2: When we look at the pictures of the women who lived in slavery, we notice that they are all dressed very similarly. They are usually wearing white scarves around their hair. Why do you think they dressed this way?

Possible answers: There are many possible reasons. One is that slaves wore a kind of uniform, and a head wrap marked a woman as a slave. In addition, most people wore some kind of hat when out in public. This head wear is also the kind of garment worn in Africa, and it was a custom that linked people to the home of their ancestors. Notice that several of the women photographed after emancipation continued to wear the white kerchiefs. Contrast most of the photographs with the portrait of Nancy Lawson (page 58)—her headwear, typical of what was fashionable at the time, indicates that she was a free woman.

Question 3: Two of the photographs (pages 11 and 49) show families sitting in front of their quilts. Why do you suppose they would hang a quilt for the family portrait?

Possible answers: The quilts may have been something that the family was proud of and wanted to show off, but it is more likely that the photographer asked them to hang some kind of a blanket to use as a backdrop. These photographs were probably taken outside to make use of the sunlight, and the photographer may not have wanted a busy background. Notice, however, that the photographer who captured the Shores family on page 98 was particularly interested in their sod house. He took many photographs of pioneers living in this kind of architecture, and he didn't want to use a backdrop to cover the view.

Question 4: Each quilt block has a name that was published in a book or magazine. Look at each block and guess why the block was given that name. For example, The First Block: Chained Star (page 29) has diamonds that look like links of a chain circling around the star. The Seventeenth Block: Beauregard Surrounded (page 86) looks like a battle plan.

Possible answers: Some of the names, like The Tenth Block: Creole Puzzle (page 58), seem to have no connection to the block. The words "Creole Puzzle" may have just sounded good. The shapes in Catch Me If You Can (page 68) seem to be running around the block.

Question 5: Nearly every block in the book has more than one name. You can come up with a new name based on what you see in the block. What is the correct name for a quilt pattern?

Possible answers: There is no correct name. Quilt pattern names are a form of folklore, which changes all the time. You can name the block anything you like. If you want your name to be remembered and become part of the folklore handed down with the quilt, you should write it on a label on the back of your quilt.

Question 6: Some people like to think that we can read old quilts like secret maps or code. Although no one has ever proven that this is the case, it's fun to think about quilts as secret codes. If you were going to use a quilt to tell a secret, how would you do it? Remember that if you use a code, someone else has to know how to read it.

Possible answers: You could sew a paper note or a map inside the quilt. Anyone who feels the paper crackling inside the quilt could rip out a few stitches and remove it. You could make a secret pocket on the back of the quilt and put a note in there. You could stitch words into the quilting stitches, where they would be hard to read. You could spell out words in Morse Code (dots and dashes) for a pieced border pattern. You could make a rebus design (a picture puzzle), like the one shown here, and stitch that into the quilting.

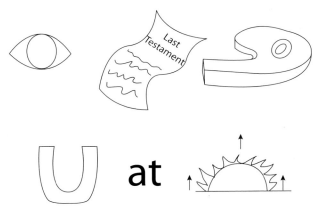

"Eye will meat U at sunrise" = I will meet you at sunrise.

Underground Railroad Doll Quilt

A First Quilt for a Young Needleworker and a Patchwork Partner

Use the Underground Railroad block to teach the basics of hand sewing as you make an 18″ × 18″ doll quilt.

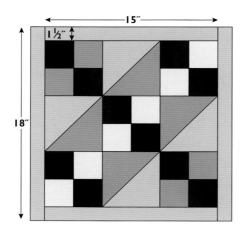

In the past, children as young as four and five were taught to make quilts. During the nineteenth century, children often learned to piece at the same time they learned to read and write. The Underground Railroad block (page 73) is excellent for use as a patchwork primer. The secret to success is for Mom or a big brother or sister to work with the young child in a team of patchwork pals. The young child works only at his or her own skill level, while the older partner helps with more complex jobs.

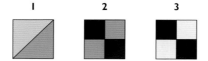

The Underground Railroad block is a nine-patch made up of two different units—a square divided into two triangles and a square made up of a four-patch, or four smaller squares. The older partner cuts and marks the pieces, sews the triangular units, pieces the units into a block, adds the border and quilts, and/or ties the finished top.

The younger partner pieces the four-patch units and assists with other steps as he or she can. Children have traditionally begun their patchwork with four-patches or nine-patches. Four-patches seem to work best for beginners, because these blocks go together fast and the older partner can cover up a multitude of errors by pressing the blocks and, if necessary, trimming them so they're square again.

Although the sewing instructions in this book use rotary cutting and machine methods—the standard sewing style adults use today—the methods are adapted here for hand sewing using a marked sewing line.

Hand sewing is an important skill to learn, one that's been taught to children for generations. As a former special education teacher, however, I'm always a little horrified by the tales I've read of an adult forcing a child to rip out the stitches if they weren't small enough or neat enough. All learning should be a positive experience. Learners need a sense of accomplishment, so the first stitches should stay in the quilt.

If the stitches are too big to hold together, you can sew over the child's seams, saying something like, "This is terrific sewing. Now I am going to go over it with a reinforcing stitch so it will be extra strong." With guidance, the next seam will be better, and you can tell the child that the stitches are getting so good you don't have to do any reinforcing stitches.

Remember that making quilts is supposed to be fun. If kids are struggling, they need more help. You know your child. Let your child do as much as possible, but make it a successful experience. Take over a job politely if it seems to be too hard. This is the first quilt—not the last.

Fabric Requirements

1 fat quarter of dark, medium, and light for block and border

Backing: 20″ × 20″

Batting: 20″ × 20″

Binding: 10″ × 20″ strip of fabric (Use the leftovers from a fat quarter.)

3 yards perle cotton to tie the quilt

1 large needle

Cutting the Doll Quilt (older partner)

Cut the borders first from the dark:

Cut 2 strips 2″ × 15½″.

Cut 2 strips 2″ × 18½″.

Marking the Squares (older partner)

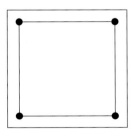

With a pencil, mark a sewing line on the back of each square. Place a dot ¼″ inside each of the corners and connect the dots with lines ¼″ inside the edge.

Hand Sewing the Squares (younger partner)

Teach the child to pin the squares face to face, with right sides together, by placing a pin in the dots and running it along the sewing line.

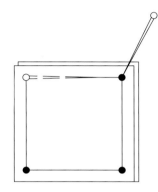

Teach the child to thread the needle and tie a knot in a double thread.

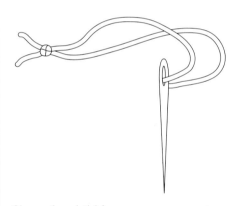

Show the child how to sew a running stitch along the pencil line. Check the other side as he or she sews to make sure the stitches stay on the line.

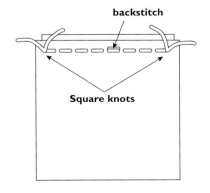

Teach the child to make a backstitch every 6 or 7 stitches to make sure the seam is strong.

The goal should probably be 6 stitches per inch measured on the top. When I taught beginning quilting to adults, I told them to aim for 8 to an inch.

Have the child remove the pins as he or she sews and put them back in the pincushion.

When the child comes to the dot, cut the thread so there is enough left to tie a knot.

Tie a square knot tightly against the fabric and trim the threads to about an inch.

Press the seams.

Congratulate the sewer before repeating the process to make 5 of the four-patch units.

Finishing the Block (older partner)

This is when the older partner has to decide if the seam is going to hold up or if it will need "reinforcement" with grown-up stitches.

If the child shows real skill and interest, she or he can stitch the triangles, using the same marking and hand stitching methods. Otherwise, the older partner can sew the 4 triangular units and assemble the block.

Press the block.

Add the side borders.

Add the top and bottom borders.

Sandwich the top, batting, and quilt.

Tie the quilt together with square knots about every 3″.

Bind.

THE ENDNOTES

1. Barbara Brackman, *Quilts From the Civil War* (Lafayette, California: C&T Publishing, 1997); Barbara Brackman, *Civil War Women* (Lafayette, California: C&T Publishing, 2000).

2. A recent summary of the conflict between myth and history in the story of Betsy Ross is included in Marc Leepson's *Flag: An American Biography* (New York: St. Martin's Press, 2005), chapter 3, pages 37–52.

3. The sources most often quoted about the Underground Railroad and quilts are the children's fictional book *Sweet Clara and the Freedom Quilt*, by Deborah Hopkinson (New York: Alfred Knopf, 1993), and two nonfiction books: *Hidden in Plain View: The Secret Story of Quilts and the Underground Railroad*, by Jacqueline L. Tobin and Raymond G. Dobard (New York: Bantam Books, 1999); and *Stitched From the Soul: Slave Quilts From the Antebellum South*, by Gladys Marie Frye (New York: E.P. Dutton, 1990).

4. James Horton, quoted in Tony Horwitz, "Department of Tourist Education," *New Yorker,* June 14, 1999, page 30. For more about the interpretation of antique quilts, see my keynote address to the American Quilt Study Group (AQSG) Seminar in 2003. "Rocky Road to Analysis: Interpreting Quilt Patterns," *Uncoverings 2004* (Lincoln, Nebraska: American Quilt Study Group, 2004), pages 1–9.

5. "Quilts of the Freedom Center," *AQSG Blanket Statements,* Fall 2004, page 4.

6. Barbara Brackman, *Encyclopedia of Pieced Quilt Patterns* (Paducah, Kentucky: American Quilters Society, 1993).

7. Press release from Sotheby's Auctions, October 13, 2000, picturing an "Important pieced and appliquéd quilt by the Enslaved African 'Yellow Bill' made for Catherine W. Dean, New Orleans, dated March, 18, 1852." The Maryland quilt, number 1945.14.1, was a gift of Mrs. William Ellicott.

8. Diary entry, January 4, 1861, in John Hammon Moore, editor, *A Plantation Mistress on the Eve of the Civil War* (Columbia: University of South Carolina Press, 1993), page 67; letter dictated by Martha, January 27, 1861, in E. Grey Dimond and Herman Hattaway, editors, *Letters From Forest Place: A Plantation Family's Correspondence, 1846–1881* (Jackson: University Press of Mississippi, 1993), pages 197–198.

9. The Works Progress Administration, later called the Works Project Administration (WPA), was part of President Franklin Roosevelt's New Deal network of federally funded initiatives to give employment to creative people, such as writers and artists, during the Great Depression. The interviews with the former slaves present several problems. For example, we can question the candor of many interviewees in their 80s who might have been intimidated by a government representative asking questions. Another problem is that the writers were instructed to transcribe the interviewee's responses in dialect. Sentences might read, "Us chillern usta play hide en seek, honey on de bee ball, frog in de meadow, an' eberthing playable. Ah learned tuh spin and ..." The sentences are difficult to read, and the tone distances and demeans the interviewee. Americans speak with a great variety of accents, but it is only the poor and disenfranchised whose words are written in dialect fashion. No one ever wrote President John Kennedy's speeches in Boston dialect. I have rewritten the interview transcriptions to reflect conventional spelling, but retained grammatical and spelling errors in people's written words.

10. Hannah Allen's interview is recorded in the most comprehensive publication of the WPA interviews, George P. Rawick's 40-volume work, *The American Slave: A Composite Autobiography* (Westport, Connecticut: Greenwood Press, 1972–1979), volume 11, number 10; Martha Colquitt interview, in Norman Yetman, *Voices From Slavery* (New York: Holt, Rinehart & Winston, 1970), page 60; Anne Bell interview, in Rawick, *The American Slave*, volume 2, page 52.

11. L.J. Coppin, *Unwritten History* (New York: Negro Universities Press, 1968), page 82; Susan Dabney Smedes, *Memorials of a Southern Planter* (Baltimore: Cushings & Bailey, 1887), page 78.

12. Claire Somersille Nolan, "The Star of Bethlehem Quilt at the Metropolitan Museum of Art," *Uncoverings 2005* (Lincoln, Nebraska: American Quilt Study Group, 2005), pages 93–199.

13. Nancy Johnson, testimony March 22, 1873, in Ira Berlin, *Slaves Without Masters: The Free Negro in the Antebellum South* (New York: Pantheon Books, 1974), page 125.

14. Diary entry, February 4, 1862, in John Q. Anderson, editor, *Brokenburn: The Journal of Kate Stone 1861–1868* (Baton Rouge: Louisiana State University Press, 1955), pages 88 and 91.

15. Robert Manson Myers, editor, *Children of Pride: A True Story of Georgia and the Civil War* (New Haven, Connecticut: Yale University Press, 1972); Robert Manson Myers, editor, *A Georgian at Princeton* (New York: Harcourt, Brace, Jovanovich, 1976), pages 65 and 335.

16. Letter, July 17, 1861, in Myers, *Children of Pride*, page 718. Fannie Moore interview, in Yetman, *Voices From Slavery*, page 227. For more about quilts and needlework by enslaved women, see Gloria Seaman Allen's studies, "Slaves as Textile Artisans: Documentary Evidence for the Chesapeake Region," *Uncoverings 2001* (Lincoln, Nebraska: American Quilt Study Group, 2001) and "Quiltmaking on Chesapeake Plantations," in *On the Cutting Edge* (Lewisburg, Pennsylvania: Oral Traditions Project, 1994).

17. Diary entry, July 11, 1810, New Brunswick, New Jersey, in Lucia McMahon and Deborah Schriver, editors, *To Read My Heart: The Journal of Rachel Van Dyke, 1810–1811* (Philadelphia: University of Pennsylvania Press, 2000), page 44.

18. Peter Corn interview, in Rawick, *The American Slave*, volume 11, page 94.

19. Richard Jones interview, in Yetman, *Voices From Slavery*, page 192.

20. Charlie Grant interview, in Rawick, *The American Slave*, volume 2, pages 172–173.

21. Thomas Clarkson, *The History of the Rise, Progress, and Accomplishment of the Abolition of the African Slave-Trade by the British Parliament* (London: Longman, Hurst, Rees and Orme, 1808), page 110.

22. Letter from Adrian, Michigan Territory, November 28, 1833, in Marcia J. Heringa Mason, editor, *Remember the Distance That Divides Us* (East Lansing: Michigan State University Press, 2004), page 210.

23. Charles W. Burkett and Clarence Hamilton Poe, *Cotton, Its Cultivation, Marketing ...* (New York: Doubleday, 1906).

24. Solomon Northup, *Twelve Years a Slave* (Auburn, New York: Debry and Miller, 1853), quoted in Alan Gallay, *Voices of the Old South, Eyewitness Accounts, 1528–1861* (Athens: University of Georgia Press, 1994), pages 334–335.

25. Betty Abernathy interview and Annie Bridges interview, in Rawick, *The American Slave*, volume 11, pages 6 and 44.

26. Frederick Ross interview, in Rawick, *The American Slave*, volume 11, page 298.

27. Frederica Bremer, *The Homes of the New World* (New York: Harper & Brothers, 1853).

28. W.C. Parson Allen interview, in Rawick, *The American Slave*, volume 11, page 18.

29. Rebecca Latimer Felton, *Country Life in Georgia in the Days of My Youth* (Atlanta, Georgia: Author, 1919), page 98.

30. Letter from Abraham Lincoln, Springfield, Illinois, August 24, 1855, in Roy P. Basler, *Abraham Lincoln: His Speeches and Writing* (Cleveland, Ohio: World Publishing Company, 1946), volume 2, page 320.

31. Frederick Law Olmsted, *The Cotton Kingdom* (London: S. Low, Son & Company, 1861), page 37; Harriett Martineau, *Society in America* (London: Saunders & Otly, 1837), page 34.

32. Georgia Baker interview, in James Mellon, *Bull Whip Days: The Slaves Remember* (New York: Weidenfeld & Nicolson, 1988), pages 6–7.

33. Aunt Sarah interview, in Rawick, *The American Slave*, volume 11, page 360.

34. Order, September 20, 1759, in Joseph E. Fields, editor, *"Worthy Partner": The Papers of Martha Washington* (Westport, Connecticut: Greenwood Press, 1994), page 88; Willis Winn interview, in Yetman, *Voices From Slavery*, page 331.

35. Frederick Douglass, *My Bondage and My Freedom* (Auburn, New York: Miller, Orton & Company, 1857; New York: Penguin Books, 2003), pages 76–77.

36. Louis Hill interview, in Rawick, *The American Slave*, volume 11, page 186.

37. Sarah Graves interview, in Rawick, *The American Slave*, volume 11, page 131.

38. Thomas B. Chaplin diary entry, May 22, 1846, St. Helena's Island, South Carolina, in Theodore Rosengarten, *Tombee: Portrait of a Cotton Planter* (New York: William Morrow & Company, 1986), page 426; Grace Brown Elmore diary entry, November 27, 1867, in Marli F. Weiner, editor, *Heritage of Woe: The Civil War Diary of Grace Brown Elmore, 1861–1868* (Athens: University of Georgia Press, 1997), page 162.

39. Dan Josiah Lockhart, quoted in Benjamin Drew, *The Refugee: A North-Side View of Slavery* [electronic resource] (Chapel Hill: Academic Affairs Library, University of South Carolina, 2000), page 47.

40. Olmsted, *The Cotton Kingdom*, page 76; Caroline Howard Gilman, *Recollections of a Southern Matron* (New York: Harper & Brothers, 1838), page 101.

41. Mary Dobyns DeHaven, "Reminscences of War Times," in *Reminiscences of the Women of Missouri During the Sixties* (Kansas City, Missouri: United Daughters of the Confederacy, 1913), page 192.

42. Eliza Madison, interview, in Rawick, *The American Slave*, volume 11, page 241.

43. Douglass, *My Bondage and My Freedom*, pages 184–186.

44. Prince Johnson interview, in Yetman, *Voices From Slavery*, page 190.

45. Letter, February 12, 1836, Edenton, North Carolina, in John W. Blassingame, *Slave Testimony: Two Centuries of Letters, Speeches, Interviews & Autobiographies* (Baton Rouge: Louisiana State University Press, 1977), pages 22–23.

46. Charity Bower, interview, in Blassingame, *Slave Testimony*, page 263.

47. Delia Garlic interview, in Yetman, *Voices From Slavery*, page 133.

48. Letter from MCF, *The American Woman*, February 1911.

49. For a summary of charm quilts, see Cuesta Benberry, "Charm Quilts," *Quilters Newsletter Magazine*, number 120, March 1980.

50. Mollie Dawson, interview. The flaw in Mollie's story, as in many memoirs, is that time muddles memory. She may have been recalling life in the 1870s, after slavery.

51. Nancy Clemens, "Grandma's Charm String," *Mother's Home Life*, November 1936, page 311.

52. Flora Kennedy Cowgill, *Never Forgotten: Memories of a Kansas Childhood* (Lawrence, Kansas: Author, 1965), pages 13–14.

53. Gus Feaster, interview, in Rawick, *The American Slave*, volume 2, page 52.

54. Richard Jones, interview, in Yetman, *Voices From Slavery*, page 192.

55. Mary Divine, interview, in Rawick, *The American Slave*, volume 11, page 102.

56. Rebecca Grant, interview, in Rawick, *The American Slave*, volume 2, page 182. James Abbot, interview, in Rawick, *The American Slave*, volume 11, number 1.

57. Fillmore Hancock, interview, in Rawick, *The American Slave*, volume 11, page 148.

58. Harriet C. Frazier, *Runaway and Freed Missouri Slaves and Those Who Helped Them, 1763–1865* (Jefferson, North Carolina: McFarland & Company, 2004).

59. Jill LePore, *New York Burning: Liberty, Slavery, and Conspiracy in Eighteenth-Century Manhattan* (New York: Alfred A, Knopf, 2005), page 24.

60. Rudolph Eickemeyer, *Down South* (New York: R.H. Russell, 1900).

61. Diary entry, April 29, 1864, in Loretta Galbraith and William Galbraith, editors, *A Lost Heroine of the Confederacy: The Diaries and Letters of Belle Edmondson* (Jackson: University Press of Mississippi, 1990), pages 120–121.

62. Berlin, *Slaves Without Masters*, pages 15, 93, 138.

63. Kate C., *The Sunny South or the Southerner at Home* (Philadelphia: G.G. Evans, 1860), page 331.

64. Diary entry, September 12, 1855, Salem, Massachusetts, in Ray Allen Billington, *The Journal of Charlotte L. Forten* (New York: Collier Books, 1953), page 74.

65. Elizabeth Buffum Chace, "My Anti-Slavery Reminscences," in Lucille Salitan and Eve Lewis Perera, editors, *Virtuous Lives: Four Quaker Sisters* (New York: Continuum, 1994), page 98.

66. Information about Elizabeth Keckley's life (also spelled Keckly) is primarily from her autobiography *Behind the Scenes or Thirty Years a Slave and Four Years in the White House* (New York: G.W. Carelton, 1868), and a recent biography, Jennifer Fleischner's *Mrs. Lincoln and Mrs. Keckly: The Remarkable Story of the Friendship Between a First Lady and a Former Slave* (New York: Broadway Books, 2003). Harriett C. Frazier also found public records of "Lizzie" Keckley as a freed woman who obtained a license to live in Missouri in May 1859.

67. Berlin, *Slaves Without Masters*, page 56.

68. Letter from Elizabeth Hobbs to her mother, April 10, 1838, in Blassingame, *Slave Testimony*, pages 20–21.

69. Carrie Hall and Rose Kretsinger, *Romance of the Patchwork Quilt in America* (Caldwell, Idaho: Caxton Publishers, 1935).

70. Eliza Potter, *A Hairdresser's Experience in High Life* (Cincinnati, Ohio: Author, 1859; New York: Oxford University Press, 1991), pages 16–19.

71. Mrs. Dunbar Rowland, *Life, Letters, and Papers of William Dunbar* (Jackson: Press of the Mississippi Historical Society, 1930).

72. John White, interview, in Yetman, *Voices From Slavery*, page 308.

73. Diary entry, March 15, 1865, Hilton Head, South Carolina, in Gerald Schwartz, editor, *A Woman Doctor's Civil War: Esther Hill Hawk's Diary* (Columbia: University of South Carolina Press, 1984), pages 119–120.

74. "The Fugitive Negro Blacksmith," *The Non-Slaveholder*, volume V (August 1, 1850), pages 183–186.

75. Account of a speech given by Samuel May Jr. at the 18th Annual Meeting of the Massachusetts Anti-Slavery Society in 1850, page 93.

76. Douglass, *My Bondage and My Freedom*, page 203.

77. Samuel Ringgold Ward, *Autobiography of a Fugitive Negro* (London: John Snow, 1855), pages 22–23.

78. Letter, December 1860, Auburn, New York, in Sherry H. Penney and James D. Livingston, editors, *A Very Dangerous Woman: Martha Wright and Women's Rights* (Amherst: University of Massachusetts Press, 2004).

79. Potter, *A Hairdresser's Experience*, pages 16–19.

80. Hugh Dunn Fisher, *The Gun and the Gospel: Early Kansas and Chaplain Fisher* (Chicago, 1896).

81. Letter, March 18, 1859, in Blassingame, *Slave Testimony*, page 114.

82. Letter, February 20, 1859, Clay-Ashland, Liberia, in Blassingame, *Slave Testimony*, page 107.

83. Douglass, *My Bondage and My Freedom*, pages 120–121.

84. Henry Brown, *Narrative of Henry Box Brown, Who Escaped Slavery in a Box ...* (Boston, 1849).

85. *The Liberator*, January 2, 1837.

86. Letter, January 17, 1837, South Natick, Massachusetts, in Milton Meltzer and Patricia G. Holland, *Lydia Maria Child: Selected Letters, 1817–1880* (Amherst: University of Massachusetts Press, 1982), page 60. The quilt's accession number is 1923.597.

87. Pat Ferrero, Elaine Hedges, and Julie Silber, *Hearts and Hands: The Influence of Women and Quilts on American Society* (Nashville, Tennessee: Rutledge Hill Press, 1996), page 72.

88. Diary entry, December 6, 1854, in Billington, *The Journal of Charlotte L. Forten*, page 65.

89. Diary entry, in James W. Cortada, editor, *Diary of Fannie Page Hume* (Orange County, Virginia: Orange County Historical Society, 1983), page 43.

90. Letter, June 28, 1862, Fortress Monroe, Virginia, in Georgeanna Woolsey Bacon, *Letters of a Family During the War for the Union* (New Haven, Connecticut: Author, 1899), pages 432–433.

91. Letter, December 30, 1862, in Virginia Jeans Laas, editor, *Wartime Washington: The Civil War Letters of Elizabeth Blair Lee* (Urbana: University of Illinois Press, 1991), page 222.

92. George Bolinger interview, in Rawick, *The American Slave*, volume 11, pages 69–70.

93. Hawk, pages 69–70 (see note 73).

94. Eliza Brown Davison told her story through Elizabeth Bacon Custer's *Tenting on the Plains* (Norman: University of Oklahoma Press, 1971), pages 26, 27, 37–48. Nancy P. Allan has found a good deal more about Davison's life for her article "Standing Up for Liberty: Eliza Brown Davison and the Custers," *Research Review: The Journal of the Little Big Horn Associates*, volume 17, number 1, Winter 2003, pages 2–12.

95. Annie Bridges interview, in Rawick, *The American Slave*, volume 11, pages 50–51.

96. Letter, January 30, 1862, in Farah Jasmine Griffin, editor, *Beloved Sisters and Loving Friends: Letters From Rebecca Primus of Royal Oak, Maryland, and Addie Brown of Hartford, Connecticut, 1854–1868* (New York: Knopf, 1999), page 59.

97. Edward Taylor, interview, in Rawick, *The American Slave*, volume 11, page 340.

98. Elmore, page 121 (see note 73). Lucy Davis interview, in Rawick, *The American Slave*, volume 11, page 101.

99. James Wilson interview, in Rawick, *The American Slave*, volume 11, page 372.

100. William Black and Mary Divine interviews, in Rawick, *The American Slave*, volume 11, page 103.

101. Louis Thomas interview, in Rawick, *The American Slave*, volume 11, page 350.

102. Letter, November 3, 1865, Concord, Massachusetts, in Edith E.W. Gregg, editor, *The Letters of Ellen Tucker Emerson* (Kent, Ohio: The Kent State University Press, 1980), volume 1, page 355.

103. Letter, May 15, 1867, in Josephine W. Martin, editor, *"Dear Sister:" Letters Written on Hilton Head Island, 1867* (Beaufort, South Carolina: Beaufort Book Company, 1977), page 83.

104. Eliza Madison and Frederick Ross interviews, in Rawick, *The American Slave*, volume 11, pages 241 and 300.

105. "Descendants Hope to Infuse New Life Into Ex-Slave Colony," *Lawrence Journal World*, August 23, 2004.

ABOUT THE AUTHOR

Barbara Brackman has written numerous books about quilts and quilt history, among them *America's Printed Fabrics: 1770–1890* for C&T Publishing. She lives in Lawrence, Kansas, a town founded by antislavery activists before the Civil War. She works as a consultant with the Kansas Museum of History, where she curated an exhibit on territorial history for the state's recent sesquicentennial anniversary. She also volunteers at the Helen Foresman Spencer Museum of Art at the University of Kansas, where she is Honorary Curator of Quilts. She was a founding member of the American Quilt Study Group and is proud to be a member of the Quilters' Hall of Fame.

Photo by Ray Rowden

THE INDEX

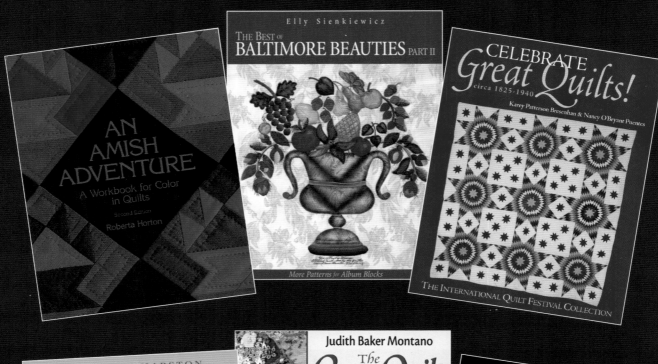